P9-DCP-212

➤ *Transforming Fire* ➤

Also by the author from Paulist Press

Autumn Gospel

Christian Foundations (Revised Edition) (with Thomas Hart)

A Counselor's Prayer Book (with Thomas Hart)

Facing Discouragement (with Thomas Hart)

The First Two Years of Marriage (with Thomas Hart)

The Inner Rainbow

Promises to Keep (with Thomas Hart)

Women at the Well

➤ *Transforming Fire* ➤

Women Using Anger Creatively

Kathleen Fischer

LIBRARY
ST. JOSEPH'S PROVINCIAL HOUSE
LATHAM, NEW YORK 12110

PAULIST PRESS
New York   Mahwah, N.J.

A
ROBERT J. WICKS
Spirituality Selection

248.8
F529t

Another Robert J. Wicks Spirituality Selection

Simply SoulStirring by Francis Dorff, O. Praem.

Cover design by Cynthia Dunne

Copyright © 1999 by Kathleen Fischer

All rights reserved. No part of this book may be reproduced or transmitted in any form or by any means, electronic or mechanical, including photocopying, recording or by any information storage and retrieval system without permission in writing from the Publisher.

Library of Congress Cataloging-in-Publication Data

Fischer, Kathleen R., 1940 –
  Transforming fire : women using anger creatively / by Kathleen Fischer.
    p. cm.
  "A Robert J. Wicks spirituality selection."
  Includes bibliographical references.
  ISBN 0-8091-3902-2 (alk. paper)
    1. Christian women—Religious life.   2. Anger—Religious aspects—Christianity. I. Title.
  BV4527.F55 1999
  248.8'43 –dc21   99-41943
                                                                    CIP

Published by Paulist Press
997 Macarthur Boulevard
Mahwah, New Jersey 07430

www.paulistpress.com

Printed and bound in the
United States of America

CONTENTS

32/65

ACKNOWLEDGMENTS

The Publisher gratefully acknowledges use of the following: Lines from "In whom we live and move and have our being" and "In Private" by Denise Levertov, from SANDS OF THE WELL. Copyright © 1996 by Denise Levertov. Reprinted by permission of New Directions Publishing Corp. and Bloodaxe Books. Lines from "Talking to Oneself" by Denise Levertov, from CANDLES IN BABYLON. Copyright © 1982 by Denise Levertov. Reprinted by permission of New Directions Publishing Corp. and Bloodaxe Books. Excerpt on rite for healing from rape from WOMEN-CHURCH: THEOLOGY AND PRACTICE OF FEMINIST LITURGICAL COMMUNITIES by Rosemary Radford Ruether. Copyright © 1985 by Rosemary Radford Ruether. Reprinted by permission of HarperCollins Publishers, Inc. Three blessings from THE BOOK OF BLESSINGS: NEW JEWISH PRAYERS FOR DAILY LIFE, THE SABBATH AND THE NEW MOON FESTIVAL by Marcia Falk. Copyright © 1996 by Marcia Lee Falk. Reprinted by permission of HarperCollins Publishers, Inc. "Portrait of a Figure Near Water," "Bright Sun after Heavy Snow," and "No," copyright © 1996 by the Estate of Jane Kenyon. Reprinted from *Otherwise: New & Selected Poems* by Jane Kenyon with the permission of Graywolf Press, Saint Paul, Minnesota. Lines from two poems reprinted by permission of the publishers and the Trustees of Amherst College from THE POEMS OF EMILY DICKINSON, Thomas H. Johnson, ed., Cambridge, Mass.: The Belknap Press of Harvard University, Copyright © 1951, 1955, 1979, 1983 by the President and Fellows of Harvard College. Excerpts from *The Power of Naming: A Concilium Reader in Feminist Liberation Theology*, edited by Elisabeth Schüssler Fiorenza. Copyright © 1996. Reprinted by permission of Orbis Books, Maryknoll, New York, and SCM Press, London, England. Lines from Mechtild of Magdeburg's poem, "A fish cannot drown in water...," translated by Oliver Davies in *Beguine Spirituality*, edited by Fiona Bowie. Copyright © 1989. Used with permission of The Crossroad Publishing Company and Burns & Oates, Ltd. Lines from Catherine de Vinck, "The Womanly Song of God," from *God of a Thousand Names*. Copyright © 1993. Used by permission of ALLELUIA PRESS, Allendale, NJ 07401. Prayer from *Celebrating Women: The New Edition*, edited by Hannah Ward, Jennifer Wild, and Janet Morley (Harrisburg, PA: Morehouse Publishing). Copyright © 1995. Used with permission of author Jennifer Wild. Lines from "The Limits Undone" by Neile Graham, from *Spells for a Clear Vision*. Copyright © 1994. Used with permission of Brick Books, London, Ontario, Canada. Excerpt from "After Auschwitz," from THE AWFUL ROWING TOWARD GOD by Anne Sexton. Copyright © 1975 by Loring Conant, Jr., Executor of the Estate. Reprinted by permission of Houghton Mifflin Co. All rights reserved.

Unless otherwise indicated, scripture quotations are from the Jerusalem Bible (New York: Doubleday & Company, 1966). Quotations designated NRSV are from the New Revised Standard Version (New York: Oxford University Press, 1989).

PREFACE

hile listening to women's stories over the years, I began to notice how many different starting points took us to the topic of anger. Whether we began with family issues or childhood memories; friendship or forgiveness; parenting, work, or prayer, we found ourselves eventually exploring kinds of anger. So I set out to discover as much as I could about women's anger, especially its spiritual dimensions, where some of the most significant and complex issues emerge. This book is my attempt to share what I have learned.

We often fear that anger is the antithesis of love. But it is actually an intrinsic, though difficult, dimension of loving well. This aspect or work of love seems more fragile and yet more urgent because of the specter of violence that hangs over civilization today. Men, as well as women, are trying to find their way in a world that both generates anger and constricts its expression. Much of what I say will therefore be useful to anyone dealing with anger. Yet, while many of our issues are similar, there are basic differences in the cultural and religious contexts of anger for women and men. These result from the messages society and religion give us about the meaning of being female or male. I try to show how these frame women's attempts to deal with anger.

It is hard at times to speak of spirituality and anger in the same breath. Are they not the antithesis of each other? In fact, anger is essential to a healthy spirituality. Losing anger's passion condemns us to the status quo. Failing to direct it wisely puts us and our world at risk. And developments in women's spirituality in recent decades have made it even more necessary to understand anger. This emerging spirituality emphasizes the importance of women's experience; the integration of body and mind, emotion and reason; the significance of connection in women's lives and of mutuality in relationships; a sense of our embeddedness in the natural world; the

1

recovery of female symbols for the sacred; and issues of power and powerlessness. Many women enthusiastically embrace the fresh insights arising from this discussion. But attempting to live them out in daily detail brings us face to face with perplexing dilemmas regarding anger. I try to address some of these.

As we study an emotion like anger more fully, it becomes clear that it is not a simple entity, but rather a complex physical, intellectual, cultural, and spiritual reality. No one discipline can interpret anger adequately. I therefore rely on a variety of approaches, including theology, psychology, and contemporary science. While I consider anger primarily from a Christian perspective, I draw as well on the resources of other spiritual traditions, especially Judaism and Buddhism. Further, since emotional truth is multifaceted and multilayered, it is best approached from many sides rather than with a single straight-on view. For that reason, I try to understand anger from different angles. In this way I hope also to create a model for women as we work with our own angers: taking one aspect at a time, circling back to look at it from different perspectives, giving ourselves the time we need to move more deeply into its implications.

Women's experiences of anger differ, and we approach it in unique ways. I have therefore designed these pages as a resource, a kind of guide to anger, which can either be read as a whole or consulted on specific topics of interest. I hope it will be useful to individual women and women's groups as well as to those who work with women in various settings.

I begin with suggestions for understanding the meaning of anger and directing its energy well. Next I treat the integration of love and anger, focusing on such areas as self-esteem, intimate relationships, receiving anger, and dealing with conflict. In the final section I discuss ways to work with anger that move us beyond the pitfalls of either muffling or venting it. This takes us into the arenas of power, creativity, violence, nonviolence, and forgiveness. I close with a meditation on women, anger, and God in the Book of Ruth.

Walking with women over the years as they courageously chose to explore their angers has been a source of insight and inspiration for me. What I have learned from the women for whom I have

2

been teacher, spiritual director, and therapist is woven throughout these pages. I am grateful to them as well as to my family and friends for all they have contributed to this book. I have changed identifying details to protect confidentiality throughout.

"I set before you life or death," we read in Deuteronomy 30:19. "Choose life, then, so that you and your descendants may live." This is what we are reaching for in a spirituality of anger: a way to harness the fire in us and all of creation, to move it toward life-giving rather than death-dealing ends. In anger thus transfigured we discover clarity, connection, power, and grace.

Section I
Naming Our Angers

1. Choosing to Feel

> One understands the persistence, now, in our fairy tales and myths, of princesses frozen or put to sleep, held under glass, locked up in towers, their life functions brought down to as low a pitch as they could be without their dying altogether.
>
> —Carol Lee Flinders
> *At the Root of This Longing*[1]

t is a sunny spring afternoon in Seattle, and outside my office window I can see the first fresh green appearing on the trees. Inside, another kind of tentative growth is apparent. I sit with Carolyn, a woman in her late forties, who is beginning to explore her fear of being angry: "I don't do anger," she says. "Anger isn't allowed. It just isn't allowed. What I learned in our family is that it just leads to fights and arguments. Anger is destructive. It's always destructive. I do a lot of emotions, but I don't do anger."

Most of us know exactly what Carolyn is trying to say and could provide a chorus of other reasons to avoid anger at all costs: We have no right or cause to be angry. It destroys relationships. We feel out of control and guilty when we're angry. It is sinful. People do not like angry women. If we let ourselves get angry, we won't know what to do with it or how to get out of it. Emotions are time-consuming and exhausting; they get in the way and keep us from being productive.

Many women learn very early how to silence their anger. In *Meeting at the Crossroads,* Lyn Mikel Brown and Carol Gilligan explain why we do this.[2] They examine the turning points in our lives as girls and women. What, on the way to womanhood, does a girl give up? Brown and Gilligan ask. They conclude that the passage out of girlhood is a journey into silence and disconnection. It is a troubled crossing, during which a girl loses a sense of self and becomes tentative and unsure. In order to preserve relationships she disowns her feelings and suppresses her experience. She learns to accommodate herself to the needs and feelings of others, especially men. Faced with a confusing array of messages about how to succeed in relationships, she concludes that the safest path is to sacrifice the self.

During the study one hundred girls were interviewed annually. At younger ages, like seven and eight, the girls are clear, honest, and outspoken about their angry feelings, but they are under great pressure to be perfect—perfectly calm, quiet, and kind. By adolescence the girls stop expressing their real feelings, especially anger. They realize that anger brings loss of popularity and personal relationships. Rather than risk this, the girls in the study deny their emotions and suppress their self-expression. The open conflict and free speaking that were part of their daily living give way to more covert forms of responding to hurt feelings and disagreements within relationships. As a result some girls come to ignore or not know the signs of emotional and physical abuse.

This self-silencing is often so complete that many women forget that it even occurred. What remains is the inability to say what we feel or to name what we see around us. The acute sense of true and false relationship, which is so clear in girls in middle childhood, erodes through adolescence under pressure to become the perfect young woman. We lose other things too. By giving up our voice, we relinquish the right to a whole range of emotional experiences and to many of our talents and personal gifts.

Reading Gilligan's research evoked an incident in my own life that has long puzzled me. For Christmas the year I was in eighth grade, my family gave me money to buy a recording of Tchaikovsky's *Nutcracker Suite*. It was one of the first pieces of classical music I came to know and love, and I had wanted my own copy for some time. As my friend Marilyn and I emerged from the record store where I had just purchased it, a man came running out of an office building, collided with me on his way to his car, and then got in and drove away. The impact of the collision knocked me to the ground, and the record broke into several pieces. Stunned and weeping, I made my way with Marilyn back to the record store to ask if they would replace it. They wouldn't. Then we went to the office of her mother, who was a nurse, to see how badly I had injured my knee, which took the brunt of the fall. It would heal. But these were scarce times for my family, and there was no money to replace the record. What confounds me each time I recall this event is that I have no memory of getting angry. No sense of outrage at what this man did to me and my record. Nothing but a deep sense of sadness and loss. I felt helpless rather than angry.

Recalling this and other incidents, I wondered: Given our troubled history with anger, can we learn to use it well? I believe two clarifications regarding the meaning of emotions provide an initial foundation for doing so.

The moral issue is not, "Are my feelings good or bad?" but "What do I do with what I feel?"

We tend to label feelings themselves as good or bad, positive or negative. In doing this, we are assigning them moral qualities. Within such a schema, anger is inevitably judged to be wrong. In fact, it comes right near the top of the seven capital sins, just after pride. Shaped by this judgment, we tell ourselves that we should not be angry. We struggle against the feeling itself. When all anger is condemned as sin, we lose the grace and power that come from anger acknowledged and integrated.

It is hard to convince ourselves that moral quality, or the judgment of right and wrong, should be applied to actions, not feelings. But this is, in fact, the case. In her now classic essay, "The Power of Anger in the Work of Love," ethicist Beverly Harrison reminds us that the command to love is not an order to *feel* a certain way. It does not create the power to *feel* love, and was never intended to do so. Feelings deserve our respect for what they are, she believes. There are no right and wrong feelings.[3]

This conviction frees us to both recognize our feelings and choose what to do with them. Anger is a vital passion, filled with energy. We know from experience that it can be used in both constructive and destructive ways; it can fuel either life-giving or death-dealing actions. We do need to take responsibility for our own capacities for evil. But trying not to feel does not position us to choose life-affirming directions. In fact, being disconnected from our anger both limits creative discernment and constricts our ability to empathize with another's feelings. Through anger, the body is giving us vital information about the quality of our connections to self, others, and the earth. Ignoring or denying its messages seriously hampers our capacity to love. Attention to all our feelings, on the other hand, enables us to accept, to heal, to change, to understand the roots of both goodness and evil.

Culture shapes both the experience and the
expression of an emotion.

Emotions include more than bodily feelings. The discoveries of the past two decades show that emotions are responses of the whole person. An emotion is a complex event that is at once spiritual, physical, rational, and cultural. It is a lived process, an interaction that draws its meaning from the body, the mind, and the world that surrounds us. For example, though anger is an embodied experience, the body does not tell us how to interpret the physical signals it sends when we are angry. Such interpretation depends not only on our personal histories, but on what society tells us about anger. In other words, emotion is socially constructed.

Gender, or the cultural experience of being female or male, is one of the factors shaping what and how we feel. Anger is constructed differently for women and men. To understand what this means, it may be helpful to look at research on an experience often confused with anger, that of aggression. Sometimes we use this term in a popular sense to describe a person as acting aggressively. But in its more precise meaning, aggression is intentional action aimed at hurting or destroying another. It may or may not be linked with anger. At times it is greed, as in the stockpiling of military weapons, that drives the destructive action. Or it may be fear that leads one to try to control another by force. When feelings of anger do express themselves in aggression, it is very different for women than for men.

Anne Campbell, a psychologist and criminologist who has

researched aggression and violent behavior for more than twenty years, believes that women and men differ in their aggressive behavior because of the social contexts in which we live. Women see aggression as a temporary loss of control caused by overwhelming pressure and resulting in guilt. Men view aggression as a means of exerting control over other people when they feel the need to reclaim power and self-esteem. Both sexes recognize an intimate connection between aggression and control, but for women aggression is the failure of self-control, while for men it is the imposing of control over others: "Women's aggression emerges from their inability to check the disruptive and frightening force of their own anger. For men, it is a legitimate means of assuming authority over the disruptive and frightening forces of the world around them."[4] In essence, for women the fear of aggression is a fear of breaking relationships; for men, it is the fear of failure, of fighting and losing, or of not being a man enough to fight at all.

Campbell's research illumines another aspect of aggression. Men's blood pressure does indeed drop after aggression against someone who has insulted them. Women's does not. This difference is due to the fact that girls learn to respond to their aggression, not with a sense of being purified and calmed, but with a sense of shame. Aggression feels good to men, but not to women.[5] Society teaches boys that aggression is a matter of interpersonal dominance. Girls learn that it is a failure of personal control.

The social context of anger includes not only gender experiences, but the larger oppression that comes with race and class. Audre Lorde, in *Sister Outsider*, makes this point powerfully regarding women of color. She says that women of color in America have grown up within a symphony of anger at being silenced and unchosen, knowing that when they survived it was in spite of a world that took for granted their lack of humanity.

> And I say *symphony* rather than *cacophony* because we have had to learn to orchestrate those furies so that they do not tear us apart. We have had to learn to move through them and use them for strength and force and insight within our daily lives. Those of us who did not learn this difficult lesson did not survive. And part of my anger is always libation for my fallen sisters.[6]

Anger is not simply a personal issue. When the boundaries of the mind and body are violated for any group, as they are in racism, all of us are deeply affected.

These two aspects of the meaning of emotion—the moral quality of feelings and actions, and the cultural nature of emotion— provide a foundation for coming to know our angers. They bring some initial freedom from the belief that all anger is sinful and dangerous, especially for women. They also prepare us to notice the ways in which gender considerations influence interpretations of our anger and its expressions. Both are pivotal to the task of integrating anger more fully into spirituality.

2. Deep Noticing

This kind of split makes me crazy, this territorializing of the holy. Here God may dwell. Here God may not dwell. It contradicts every-thing in my experience, which says: God dwells where I dwell. Period.

—Nancy Mairs
Ordinary Time[1]

olly, a woman in her early thirties, is troubled by the fact that she has no close friendships. "When I meet someone, things seem great at first," she says, "but over time it never goes anywhere. Things just sort of go dead." I ask her if she ever gets angry with these friends. No, Molly replies, she seldom feels any anger. Sometimes she is numb, almost anesthetized, after a con-versation with her friend Karen, like being shot full of Novocain at the dentist's. After such exchanges she feels distant from her and critical of almost everything Karen does, but she does not think of herself as angry.

If you have experiences like Molly's, you might ask yourself:

Do I have a hard time knowing when I am angry? When people ask me if I am angry do I say no when I really am?

Am I often afraid to say what I really think or feel because I believe people will be uncomfortable or not like me?

Do anger and conflict frighten me? Do I try to avoid them at all costs?

Do I think of anger as an ugly part of me, something that keeps me from being holy, good, and close to God?

13

Given the problematic nature of anger, it might seem best simply not to feel it at all. But anger silenced is not benign. We may seethe inwardly, only to blow up later. Eventually we can feel so full of anger that it seems dangerous to tap it. When we finally do, it may come out in exaggerated or ineffective forms, in screaming and yelling and then endless apologies. Or it may never get expressed directly, and be turned into bodily symptoms or self-hatred. All its positive power is then lost from the pursuits and projects that could embrace it. Harriet Lerner reminds us in *The Dance of Anger* that "the amount of creative, intellectual, and sexual energy that is trapped by this need to repress anger and remain unaware of its sources is simply incalculable."[2]

Expressions of anger can also become quite convoluted: We are silent and withdrawn, hoping the other person will notice how steamed we are. We smile while making a cutting remark. Or we accuse and attack on other topics. These approaches do not satisfy us because they are not about the real sources of pain. If we are to integrate our anger with love, we need to learn to undertake real engagement with difficult feelings.

Many indirect expressions of anger develop in relationships where our experience is not heard and valued. People forced to adjust to an inferior status devise accommodating behaviors. When we feel invisible, when our experience is not heard and responded to, then the pain comes out in other ways. The anger wears a disguise. It may be such a clever disguise that we ourselves gradually no longer recognize the anger. Withdrawing, criticizing, undermining—these are some of the indirect forms anger can take. They alert us to the hidden anger we may not be acknowledging in ourselves or others.

How can we recover a clear sense of our anger? If our primary style of anger is to deny or repress it, we need a spiritual practice that connects us with it again. One helpful approach to letting ourselves feel anger is the Buddhist practice of awareness or mindfulness.

Practicing Awareness

There is nothing intrinsically Buddhist about mindfulness. It can be, and is, practiced by those of many different spiritual traditions.

Think of mindfulness as a deep noticing, a simple focus on present experience as revealing the divine, a practice that also brings about greater calm, compassion, and self-acceptance.[3] Mindfulness encourages us to let something simply *be*, without judgment. It asks us to become an impartial witness to our experience: "Yes," we say to ourselves, "this is how it is. This is how I am feeling."

Such nonjudgmental awareness is difficult because an internal critic is ever active, telling us what we *should* and *should not* feel. Each of us has such a critic ready to insult us and tell us what is wrong with us. At the first stirrings of anger, it is likely to kick in with comments such as: "I really shouldn't let this be bothering me." "It won't do me any good to get angry." "You're so stupid to have let this happen."

Because anger has been hard for women, we are more likely to spend time talking to ourselves than listening to ourselves. In *Silencing the Self,* Dana Jack uses the term "Over-Eye" to represent these moral "shoulds." She distinguishes it from an authentic "I." The "Over-Eye" names the way we internalize outer expectations and then conform to them in order to gain approval or be seen as good. Instead of arising from our own feelings and expressing them, it feels like a person outside and above us lecturing us, attacking us, criticizing us. Because the judgments of the "Over-Eye" express culture's norms about feminine goodness, truth, and value, they can override the authentic self's viewpoint.[4]

But thoughts that deny us a right to our anger are not helpful. Often an emotion is not as troublesome as the shoulds and should-nots we repeat to ourselves. We patronize our emotions and treat them like unruly children who need to be disciplined. The trail of this kind of talk usually leads to bad feelings about ourselves. By the time this inner voice finishes attacking us for even having the feeling, we have lost what it was. In its place we feel shame and guilt. All creative inner work, including the creative use of anger, depends on putting this critical voice to one side while we listen fully to what is happening in us.

Mindfulness helps us do that. In contrast to this judging voice, awareness allows us simply to acknowledge anger. We no longer chase it away, hate it, or fear it. We stop doing violence to ourselves by trying to fight or destroy the anger, and begin treating it with love and care. Mindful awareness simply sees, accepts, and is present, even when we know there are other ways we could feel. It is self-empowering because it permits self-knowledge without the constant presence of an ideal against which we inevitably fall short. The foundations of mindfulness sutra describes the activity of mindfulness in this way: "When anger is present, one knows: 'Anger is in me,' or when anger is not present, one knows: 'There is no anger in me.'" What mindfulness does not do is go on to make the judgment "I am wrong to have this anger."[5] It allows all of our competing voices to be heard. Being aware of confusion in ourselves relieves us of the strain of fighting it or pretending it is not there.

From the time we are very young, we need people who can join us in the full range of our feelings. When this does not happen we begin to ask ourselves: Is there something wrong with feeling angry? What does that mean? Is there something wrong with me? In time these questions become confused with the anger, and we no longer know what our experience is. I think that is why the following passage in Judith Duerk's *Circle of Stones: Woman's Journey to Herself* evokes something akin to nostalgia in many women. Like media images of the perfect holiday gathering, it suggests a kind of original innocence we long to recreate. Perhaps it also shows us a fresh way of listening to feelings of anger.

How might it have been different for you, if, early in your life, the first time you as a tiny child felt your anger coming together inside yourself, someone, a parent or grandparent, or older sister or brother, had said, "Bravo! Yes, that's it! You're feeling it!"

If, the first time you experienced that sharp awareness of ego, of "me, I'm me, not you"...you had been received and hugged and affirmed, instead of shamed and isolated.

If someone had been able to see that you were taking the first tiny baby step toward feeling your own feelings, of knowing that you saw life differently from those around you. If you had been helped to experience your own uniqueness, to feel the excitement of sensing, for the very first time, your own awareness of life. What if someone had helped you to own all of this...to own your own life?[6]

Another helpful way to become better acquainted with our anger is to keep an anger journal. This enables us to collect information on our anger until we get to know it better. In the journal, record who or what made you angry, how you reacted initially, the various colorings your anger passed through, what you did with the anger, and how long you stayed upset. A journal builds emotional awareness. Keeping a journal may seem like too much trouble, but actually it takes less time and energy than we frequently expend on headaches, arguments, cut-offs, sleepless nights, and other ineffective emotional strategies.

With the help of a journal, we gradually recognize patterns not noticed before: whether we are angry more often with men or women, strangers, family members or friends; whether we yell, blame, shut down, fume, withdraw, or criticize ourselves when we are angry; how it gets expressed in food or cigarette cravings, headaches or other bodily symptoms; and whether we let go of it quickly or tend to hang on to it and relive the incidents over and over in our minds. Journaling will also help us identify the relationship of our anger to PMS or other cycles, transitions, work changes or grief. Women who cannot find words for the anger sometimes like to make a collage of it, cutting out and pasting together images of it. That gets the anger outside and makes it visible.

Since anger is related to what we value, it is helpful to notice why someone's words or actions threaten us: Do they insult me or call into question my skills and competency? Do they humiliate me or dismiss me because I am a woman? Do they contradict my beliefs or undermine my character?

Journaling not only teaches us about our anger style. It helps us name the emotion, express it in a safe way, and reach some clarity about what we want to do with it. The writer and activist Virginia Woolf says that faithfully recording her anger in her diary enabled her to use its energy in the melting down process she called "incandescence." Then when her anger was expressed, it had more fire and less smoke.[7] Boiling down roiling emotions helps reduce them to their essence.

Awareness of our own feelings leaves us less dependent on others' attention and opinions. We become fully alive and more grounded in that aliveness. Such awareness is a kind of self-empathy, the ability to see and understand our own experience with greater fullness, truth, and compassion.[8] Since this kind of acceptance flows from engagement with another who is empathic with our experience, initially more empathic than we are, it can be an important fruit of prayer.

Does anger separate us from God? Or can we come to see anger as a gift, without which we could not hear a call to care for ourselves and others? Anger is less frightening when seen as the Spirit's movement within us. We have learned to distrust our deepest feelings and intuitions, yet they are one way we know the Divine is at work in us.

Recently I asked a Quaker woman what her Friends Tradition might teach me about dealing with anger. She replied: "We're not very good at anger. We see ourselves as a peaceful people. But if I were to talk about dealing with it, I would say that it is part of coming into God's presence with all that we are, being real in that presence." How can we live a life in God's presence if we cannot take our anger there, knowing it will be fully embraced? Denise Levertov expresses this wonderfully in her poem, "In Whom We Live and Move and Have Our Being." She speaks of God as "the air enveloping the whole globe of being. It's we who breathe, in, out, in, the sacred...." She concludes:

> But storm or still,
> numb or poised in attention,
> we inhale, exhale, inhale,
> encompassed, encompassed.[9]

3. Emotional Intermissions

> Anger, the inner arsonist,
> held a match to her brain.
> —Jane Kenyon
> "Portrait of a Figure Near Water"[1]

n *The Alchemy of Illness*, the moving account of her struggle with chronic fatigue syndrome, Kat Duff describes a ritual she developed. She says that when the snarl gets the better of her and she is so upset, wound up or knotted with rage, sorrow, or regret that she is unable to rest, she walks down into the pasture in front of her house. There she finds a place where the cows have trampled a path, making a soft bed of dirt, and she lies down face flat on the earth. She goes down slowly, she says, first to her knees, as in prayer, then on all fours, like an animal. Finally she stretches herself out like a snake until her stomach rests on the belly of the earth.

Lying there, with her face and fingers in the dirt, she empties herself out into the earth with whispers and tears until she finally comes to rest and her breathing returns to normal. Then she becomes aware of her surroundings. She hears the calls and sees the shadows of crows circling overhead. She feels the wind on her back, smells the scents of smoke and sage it carries, hears the stream running with snowmelt from the mountains, and watches the labor of ants hauling food back to their queens. Eventually she is able to remember all the most important things she had once known and has since forgotten about her life.[2]

Duff is describing what I call an emotional intermission, some kind of pause during which we process the physical energy of an emotion before making decisions or taking action. Nothing has been more helpful to me in dealing with my own anger than this interval for getting clear and grounded. My anger is usually strong and quick, and my first impulse is to blow away the opposition. Taking time to move this initial energy has made for much better choices.

Though we are led to believe we are all wired alike emotionally, there is no standard way to feel. Recognizing that there are different ways to experience anger allows us to cope in a way that suits us personally. Two characteristic styles of anger are generally described as holding anger in or venting it—anger in or anger out. Our focus here is on the anger out style. If this is our usual style, we do not ordinarily have trouble knowing we are angry; our problem is learning good ways to work with it. My friend Sarah, for example, finds herself angry much of the time and is embarrassed and troubled by the way she lets it fly at everyone from grocery store clerks to colleagues at work. Her anger is perpetually close to the surface, strong and hard to contain, like the beating blades of a jet propelling her forward. You may be like Sarah. Ask yourself:

Do I feel angry a lot of the time or feel like I'm going to explode because of all the anger I am carrying?

Do I frequently vent my anger with mate, children, friends?

Are my relationships marked by a lot of fighting, blaming, complaining, and nagging?

Does life feel like a continual confrontation with and defending of myself against the world?

Anger rises when we sense an offense against ourselves or those we care about. Because anger is meant to mobilize us and provide strength and endurance in such emergencies, it brings about extensive and profound changes in the body. Blood supply is increased to the brain and large muscles of the body, but reduced to the digestive tract, which is not needed in an emergency. Heart rate and blood pressure rise. Powerful hormones move into the bloodstream and markedly change our metabolic activity. We feel ready to fight, to deal with danger. It is hard to think about resolving conflict when our pulse is racing and our muscles are tense.

20

In Chinese medicine, emotions such as anger are seen simply as energy. When we constrict this energy, we begin to feel smaller. We breathe less; our muscles tighten. We may need to do this initially or in some circumstances, but as a lifelong practice, it will take its toll on the body. All that held energy will begin to show up in other ways. Our goal is to allow this energy to move forward, to become life-energy. This means finding ways to process some of it without harming ourselves or others.

1. Ask for a time out.

This can be helpful when we are in any kind of personal exchange, for example, a marital fight, where we feel our anger escalating and know we are on the edge of saying things we will regret. When Sally, a client of mine, learned that her daughter was moving to Montana to live with a boyfriend who was out of work, she was so furious that she took five full days before she could respond to the news her daughter had left on her answering machine.

If we cannot count on technology to create that kind of distance, we can simply say, "I'm feeling too angry right now to continue. I'm going to take a break and we can come back to this later." What we might actually say will probably sound less composed, but still make the point that this is not a good time to be talking.

2. Breathe.

Deep breathing is an approach that can be done anywhere and takes only a moment or two. It can be used if we come upon one of our kids smearing crayons on a recently wallpapered room, or when a boss reprimands us for something a coworker failed to do. Breathing calms us and allows us to pause. Taking slow, deep breaths reduces the flood of "fight-or-flight" symptoms, slows the pulse rate and relaxes the muscles. Start by breathing through your nose. Then say "One" to yourself, and slowly inhale for at least three seconds. Pause and think, "Relax." Then exhale for three seconds. At the end of the exhale, pause and say "Two," inhale again, and so on. Try a phrase such as: "Breathing in, I see myself as a mountain. Breathing out, I feel solid." Repeat the words *mountain* and *solid* as you inhale and exhale.[3]

Calming is not the same as repressing; we are not pretending that the anger does not exist. We pause in order to be able to confront problems more effectively. If we stay in the eye of the storm, it may be too dangerous. Deep breathing takes us to other levels from which we can better assess what to do. If we practice conscious breathing at other times, it will be more readily available in moments of strong emotion.

3. Do some physical activity.

This dissipates high levels of adrenaline in the system. Almost any kind of activity will help: aerobics, weight lifting, martial arts, yoga, tennis, running, vigorous walking, swimming, biking, hiking, hitting balls, drumming, housecleaning, gardening.

One woman developed a chant that she repeats while bicycling several miles: "A way through this exists; I can find and follow it." She says she returns exhausted but feeling cleansed. A swimmer forms a fist and punches it into the water with each stroke, saying: "The water splashes all over, but my rage is hidden in it." Another used her anger following an ugly divorce to develop a garden that was the envy of her neighborhood. Gardening is also a legacy one young woman received from her beloved grandmother, who told her: "If you put your hands in the soil, just about everything will be better in an hour or two."

A woman who can remember being filled with rage from the time she was four says that physical activity has enabled her to change her pattern of throwing tantrums: "By the time I entered adolescence, I was freaking out. Sports saved me. My tantrums would have controlled my life if it hadn't been for the concentration and refocusing techniques I learned from gymnastics. My work on the balance beam helped me to steady my emotional life. I put rage into back handsprings. I played field hockey with a vengeance. On the tennis court, I *had* to win. I would grunt out my rage on my serves, like Monica Seles."[4]

4. *Meditate.*

Meditation can help us tolerate and contain anger rather than impulsively express it or try to avoid it. It helps with anger because it reduces stress. It also clarifies our vision, deepens a receptive rather than reactive disposition, and increases a sense of being interconnected with all of life. Meditation not only calms us; it centers our energies.

In a simple form of meditation, we choose a word—such as *Love, Spirit, Peace, Trust, Ocean*—which is said over and over while sitting quietly in a relaxed position, eyes closed, breathing in a regular rhythm. If other thoughts come to mind, we simply return to the word or phrase.

5. *Confide in someone you trust.*

Confiding, something we do naturally as women, is actually very useful in sorting out the information found in the emotion of anger. Talking about it with someone we trust, who will not feed our anger, is one of the best ways to gain insight into our emotions: What happened? Why? What is upsetting about it? How can we respond to it? When no one is available to talk to, one woman tapes her angry rantings and then plays them back.

Recently Maria told me about a visit with her mother, who is in her eighties and in declining health. Though Maria was not feeling well and had set aside other pressing items to get to her mother's, she was greeted on her arrival by a barrage of familiar accusations about what she had failed to do for her. "I wanted to grab my mother and just shake her," she said. "But I said to myself, 'This is my mother; I can't do that.' So, I excused myself, took the phone to the bathroom, and called up a friend. I talked and cried until I could go back and face my mother again."

6. *Use distraction.*

Sometimes it helps to do something else: Bake bread, read the newspaper, watch a movie. However, if we are inwardly sulking or plotting revenge during this time, the anger will intensify. Anything that takes us out of the trap of the moment and transposes us to a wider perspective helps. Try imagining yourself on a hillside overlooking the city until your house and your problem become just one small part of a much larger landscape.

7. Let yourself cry.

Research on women's anger reveals that crying is one of the most common ways of expressing it. Tears are a healthy release of anger.

This is true even though we may be uncomfortable with crying. Tears have been an adaptive strategy for women. We learn early on that those in power are not as threatened by tears as they are by anger. Tears bring release without physical injury or public condemnation. They discharge tension but make no political statement. Those in power, often men, mistakenly think that the tears are a sign of remorse and contrition rather than frustration and rage. Though we often equate crying with weakness or loss of control, emotional tears contain chemicals that can strengthen the immune system's response to stress. They are cleansing and therapeutic.[5]

8. Write a letter you will never send.

One way to safely release emotional energy is to write a letter to the person with whom you are angry, knowing that you will not send it. It may be necessary to do this several times before the initial energy subsides. In the process, the key issues get refined and clarified. In the end, you may choose never to actually write the person, or you may have a version of the letter you can effectively send. Some women find it helpful to tear up the letter, save the shredded versions, burn them, and mix the ashes with soil to plant seeds symbolizing the new life they hope will come from the event.

9. *Know how to practice restraint when necessary.*

Sometimes the strength of our rage is so powerful that it takes great resolve and strength to hold it in check. In her novel *Men and Angels,* Mary Gordon describes how one of her main characters, Anne, rescues her children, Peter and Sarah, from falling through the ice and drowning in a pond near their house. Laura, the young woman entrusted with their care, is sitting behind a rock reading. The children tell Anne that they asked if it was okay to go out on the ice and Laura just nodded and smiled, and didn't seem to be paying attention.

As Anne prepares to confront Laura with the neglect of her children, Gordon recounts for us how it takes her only seconds to get to the rock where Laura is sitting, how she keeps her fist clenched so she will not strike her, how her voice feels like a knife as she speaks. She waits for Laura to reply, and when she says nothing, emotion surges through Anne.

> The desire to put her hands around Laura's throat, to take one of the large rocks on the shore and smash her skull, to break the ice and hold her head under the water till she felt her life give out was as strong as any passion Anne had ever known. As strong as her love for her children, for her husband, stronger than the things that made the center of her life was her desire to inflict damage on the smiling face of this girl who might have let her children die.[6]

Anne does none of these things. Instead she tells Laura that she can no longer care for her children and must leave their house. But in Gordon's depiction, we see the strength of feeling and the restraint that is sometimes required.

Containment is a way of holding emotion, with awareness, until we can find an appropriate time and way to express it. It flows from a practice of acknowledging and working with the energy of our anger in smaller, daily ways. Then, if such strong restraint is ever asked of us, we are familiar with both what we feel and ways to deal with it safely.

Sometimes containment consists simply in finding ways to pray our way through encounters with difficult people, where showing our anger directly would not be helpful. In working with a woman pastor around conflict in her church, we developed a method of strengthening her when she was confronted by angry parishioners. She chose a symbol to carry in her pocket; in her case it was a polished agate that symbolized a favorite image of God as her rock and salvation. It felt solid and centering to her. When she met a parishioner at coffee, she held the agate in her pocket to remind her that she could get through the encounter.

4. Body and Mind

> The Heart is the Capital of the Mind—
> The Mind is a single State —
> The Heart and the Mind together make
> A single Continent—
> —Emily Dickinson[1]

oya, a vibrant woman in her thirties, is describing for me how she suddenly saw her former husband as she pulled into the grocery store parking lot: "My whole body began to tremble. I looked out the window at him and thought, 'I hate you. I hate what you did to me.'" Even now, as she tries to talk about it, the incident registers in Moya's entire being. Body and mind, emotion and intellect are all intertwined in her response.

Many past spiritualities pitted the body and emotions against mind and reason. In this scheme emotion was inferior and less trustworthy. Philosophers like René Descartes compared feelings to pets in the house of the master, Reason. They are to be subdued, like all other powers of nature. Raised on a steady diet of such beliefs, we learned to ignore the sensations and revelations our bodies continually generate. We came to see reason as existing in a separate part of the mind, where emotion should not be allowed to intrude.

Such dualism no longer prevails unchallenged. A fresh way of viewing the body/mind relationship is emerging. Mutual exchange rather than mastery and subordination is the pattern we are reaching for in all relationships, including that between mind and body. This, in turn, provides new perspectives on emotions such as anger.

How, then, are we to think about anger in a world in which body and mind are inseparable allies, when we no longer see mind as residing in the head, but as permeating the entire body?

27

Can we return reason to its roots in emotion and the body? Can we learn to think with our whole bodies? The answer starts with a new appreciation of the body.

Bodily Knowing

One of the striking things about Jesus is how concerned he is about people's bodily well-being. Hunger. Thirst. The body's ills and afflictions. All these evoke his compassion. In fact, the body is central to the gospel message. In Mark 5:24-34, for example, we read of a woman with a flow of blood. As she reaches out to touch Jesus' garment and finds her own physical condition shift, we learn that the body is not something shameful to be ignored, but a dynamic field of energy through which she relates to Jesus and Jesus to her. Reading the gospels leaves one wondering just how we could have allowed the Christian message to become anti-body.

But the truth is, most women are disconnected from their bodies in some way. A first step toward changing this is to pay attention to what your body feels like at any moment. Are parts of it numb? Do you feel tired, or like crying? Are emotions like anger connected to certain parts of your body? Sit with your symptoms; listen to the wisdom of your body. This means setting aside the suspicion you may have of things that originate there. A week after having angioplasty for a sudden and serious artery blockage, a woman is finally alone. Throughout her body she now feels the pains and stresses of that surgery; her body seems strange and unfamiliar to her. She interprets these feelings in a negative way as "neurotic." "Are there other ways," I ask, "to hear these messages from your body? What if you were able to assess, free of judgment, your body's signals about what it needs to heal and recover?"

How do we learn to listen to the body? We begin with small steps. "My doctor told me I had to stop swallowing my anger. I didn't even realize I was angry, but now I've started to think about it. I thought about all the roles I'd invented for myself—I was the perfect daughter, the superteacher, and the benevolent caretaker; I was the glue that held my dysfunctional family together."[2] As women, we may keep our anger from awareness by locking it in our jaws, plugging it up in sinus passages, or holding it in our throats. It is also helpful to notice how we move our bodies through space. How ready are we to take up space? Notice how you walk or step into a room. When you have a few moments at home or on a walk, try expanding your movements so that you have more sense of your body expanding its space. Take longer strides when walking, firmer steps on entering a room, more solid posture when standing.

Our bodily tissues have feelings, thoughts, and memories. What we know and remember is encoded there. "So when the part of your mind that is your uterus talks to you, through pain or excessive bleeding, are you prepared to listen to it?" asks physician Christiane Northrup in *Women's Bodies, Women's Wisdom*.[3] If something is happening and we try to say we feel fine, the body will tell us whether that is, in fact, true. Often in listening to women in spiritual direction or therapy, I ask them to center and attend to what is happening in their bodies right then. There is something calming about this very attention. It is most helpful when accompanied by deep breathing. A woman knows very soon if anger is lodged in her stomach, or fear is rising in her throat: "For me rage had always been like an amoeba, a primitive substance coursing through my body that took many shapes and forms. When I was younger, it was an alien being that ruled my life. Now it's the signal that something's wrong."[4] When we begin to tune into the emotion in our muscles and tissues, it is possible to feel all the parts of our body recoiling from something in fear or dread, moving toward an object with intense desire, or tightening as we prepare to ward off an attack. This deeply physical quality of emotions is part of the reason why making sounds—singing, wailing, deep sobbing—is an important part of emotional release.

There are other ways to honor bodily knowing. Read poetry. Listen to music. Paint and draw. Dance. Try massage, yoga, or tai chi. Sometimes poetry will provide words for what we cannot say, as when Anne Sexton writes in "After Auschwitz,"

> Anger,
> as black as a hook,
> overtakes me.[5]

Or, as Denise Levertov says in "Talking to Oneself,"

> Try to remember, every April, not this one only
> you feel you are walking underwater
> in a lake stained by your blood.
>
> When the east wind rips the sunlight
> your neck feels thin and weak, your clothes
> don't warm you.[6]

Poets and musicians speak in images and sounds, language that lies near emotion; they give shape to what we struggle to articulate. Artists express what does not fit easily into reason's categories. They celebrate human sensuality, showing us how feeling joins us to the world.

This way of living in the body is profoundly incarnational. It is being articulated by Latin American women theologians who tell us that the movement of the Spirit calls us all to life in this body. For example, María Pilar Aquino, in *Our Cry for Life,* highlights the importance of desire. She describes a spirituality that rejects a cold and cerebral faith and embraces one that combines passion with compassion, a struggle for justice with joy and celebration.[7]

Anger in Dreams

Our dreamworld may be the place where our anger hides out. Dream images portray bodily feelings in vivid and dramatic ways, showing us the direction of our unacknowledged emotional energy. Often anger that has been denied shows up in dreams in the form of violent or destructive images. They strip away all the cover we use, and show us what we really feel about ourselves, God, and the world.

Since anger is a self-preservation energy, it sometimes comes in dreams as fire, explosions, fighting. These are not to be taken literally; the feelings will not destroy everything if they come out. Dreams are dramatic and often use powerful imagery. They can be frightening, especially if the feelings have been long suppressed and the image is strong. But when we let ourselves feel them consciously, they may say something quite bearable, like: Get out of my life. Leave me alone. I want my space.

In the quest to learn to understand and use anger, dreams can be a powerful ally. A friend shared the following dream with me in a letter:

> I am still discovering what contributes to overload. Because for me, it is not physical busyness usually—or not that alone—but emotional or psychological overload. It kind of sneaks up on me gradually until I reach a saturation point. I had a dream last week that illustrates that.
>
> This is what I wrote when I woke up: This wild elephant starts wrecking the house. He is huge, and he also has his mate and an offspring with him. I try to get the occupants to safety in another building in the basement. But the elephants follow. It's not possible to get away from them. They will follow wherever we go. I must do something. I get people to go to another building, but the elephants follow. I don't know where else to go so the people won't be hurt by the destructive elephants. The elephants seem unstoppable. I feel helpless. I don't know what to do. I feel paralyzed, and yet it feels like my responsibility to stop them or to protect the people from them.
>
> I decided to dialogue with the elephant, asking why he was doing this. Was he hungry? Angry? What did he want? What did he hope to accomplish? The elephant said: "I am angry! I want to destroy! I feel thwarted and I won't stop this destruction until I'm pacified or until I use the energy from my frustration." When I ask, "Why me? Why my home?" the elephant responds: "Because you won't listen to me unless I go on a rampage. You ignore me. And not until I make a scene will you pay attention to me or acknowledge my presence."
>
> And then the elephant goes on to say all that he is angry about: "You don't acknowledge that you hate your job....You're angry about relationships. You just keep pretending that everything is fine. You're TOO NICE!"

In working with anger in dreams, it helps to notice what appears in the dream that we usually suppress or reject in ourselves: What in the dream do we despise? What do we most want to get away from? What in the dream threatens us? Then we open to the possibility that something we need could come from that side, though we may not know at first exactly what that is.[8]

Emotions as a Basis for Moral Action

As we saw earlier, body and mind are in constant communication, each shaping and responding to the other. Not only do thoughts evoke emotions; emotions can actually create thoughts. Every thought as well as every emotion has a biochemical equivalent. We may distrust the power contained in our deepest and nonrational knowledge, but no insight can bypass the body. Further, if we deny our own feelings and needs, we cannot respond appropriately to those of others; in fact, we are likely to treat others exactly as we treat ourselves.

Today science, traditionally regarded as the defender of reason and objectivity, is offering us a new appreciation of the place of emotions in our lives. Even in the realm of what we consider the most rational decisions and actions, feelings count as much—and often more—than reason. In a fascinating study of emotion, reason, and the human brain, neurologist Antonio Damasio shows us why emotions are not a luxury, but essential to rational thinking. In *Descartes' Error,* Damasio takes us on a journey of scientific discovery starting with the case of Phineas Gage, a construction foreman who in 1848 survived a freak accident in which an iron rod, three and one-half feet in length, passed through his head. Gage emerged as a cool, nonemotional, intelligent human being. All the abilities usually considered necessary and sufficient for rational behavior remained intact in him: knowledge, attention, memory, language. Only one thing was changed: his ability to experience feelings. But impaired feelings caused a profound defect in decision making. He could no longer anticipate the future and plan accordingly. He lost his sense of responsibility toward himself and others.

Damasio's research has continued with modern-day neurological patients affected by brain damage. It shows that the absence of emotion and feeling can break down rationality and make wise decision making almost impossible. Far from interfering with rationality, feelings serve as internal guides, and they help us communicate to others the signals that can also guide them. As Damasio concludes, "Our most refined thoughts and best actions, our greatest joys and deepest sorrow, use the body as a yardstick."[9] What he found in his patients was that their decisions were so poorly made because they had lost access to their emotional learning. Or, as a woman who was unable to access her emotions said to me: "I've lost my radar; I have no sense of direction."

Questioning Our Interpretations

Just as thoughts arise from the body, so what we think influences our emotional well-being. The conversations we carry on in our heads have a well-documented impact on our bodies. We all talk to ourselves constantly. For the most part this self-talk is a stream of injunctions and admonitions: "Do this." "You shouldn't have done that." "What were you thinking when you said that?" Within each of us are many competing voices that represent various facets of ourselves; these voices are usually carrying on an internal dialogue, and, frequently enough, a quarrel.

Our self-talk tells us how we are interpreting an experience, what thoughts we are having about it. The strength of our anger generally rises or falls according to the meaning we give events: "You get yourself into a certain imaginative place—a perception of how things are. Turns out that isn't how they are at all." When we are hurt, we defend ourselves in many ways. We split our experiences of self and other into good and bad. We isolate or deny feelings or thoughts. We run together thoughts or feelings that are separate. For example, viewing another person's words or actions as a personal offense increases anger. This is one factor in the contemporary phenomenon known as road rage. Another driver cuts in front of us in traffic and we see it as a personal insult. But the experience is open to other interpretations. That driver may be just as stressed and distracted as we are. Reminding ourselves of that usually decreases the irritation we feel.

The inner voice may also work against us by fueling our anger. It gathers all possible evidence that we have been wronged, shores it

LIBRARY
ST. JOSEPH'S PROVINCIAL HOUSE
LATHAM, NEW YORK 12110

up with past examples, and gives it the worst possible interpretation. As Jane Kenyon says in her poem, "Bright Sun After Heavy Snow,"

> Again I recall a neighbor's
> small affront—it rises in my mind
> like the huge banks of snow along the road:
> the plow, passing up and down all day,
> pushes them higher and higher....[10]

Suppose your supervisor calls you in to discuss some inadequacies in a project you have just completed. As you leave the meeting, or perhaps even during it, you are saying to yourself: "He's never liked anything I've ever done." "He wouldn't dare treat anyone else this way." This assessment of the situation may or may not be accurate, but firing up the imagination in this way puts us at risk for action that may ultimately be destructive to us. There is always a certain amount of ambiguity in human interacting. We do not fully know what others are thinking, feeling, and intending. We may believe we have been offended when no offense was intended. Or we may fail to see that an offense was intended and not feel angry when we should.

Our spontaneous initial thoughts can also be violent and murderous, filled with ways of repaying the person for the harm he or she has done to us: "I'd like to strangle her." "I'm going to see to it that he loses his job." One woman who was feeling lots of anger toward a friend found herself plotting ways to destroy her career. "These evil fantasies!" she exclaimed. "I hope they are helping me process the anger. I know I do not ever want to enact them." But beliefs generate feelings. The fuel we use to feed our anger determines whether it will create or destroy.

The conviction that distressing emotions result from the personal meaning we give negative events is central to an approach called cognitive therapy.[11] This therapy works with anger by helping us change our beliefs. Cognitive therapists suggest that our thinking can be distorted in several ways: (1) *Selective abstraction,* in which we ignore contradictory and better evidence, thus forming conclusions on the basis of an isolated negative detail. A friend fails to call on time and we decide that she doesn't really enjoy being with us. (2) *Arbitrary inference,* in which a negative appraisal is made in the absence of evidence. We see a coworker putting in extra time and effort and decide she is after our job. (3) *Overgeneralization,* in which a negative conclusion is drawn from a single event and inappropriately applied to dissimilar situations. We have a bad class and conclude that we are a failure as a teacher. (4) *Magnification,* in which the significance of a negative event is overestimated or magnified. We do not get invited to a wedding and conclude that no one likes us and we have no friends. (5) *All-or-nothing thinking,* in which we think in absolutes—everything is either good or bad, mostly the latter.

When we experience the emotions connected with both old and new ways of thinking, it becomes clear how we can work ourselves up into a frenzy that is not warranted by the events. This is why emotional catharsis without understanding is not enough to produce change. We may need to revise our inner scripts. One way to do this is to leave open the possibility of more benign and less threatening ways of interpreting an incident. A person may be out to get us, but we may also have misunderstood what they were saying. This is not the same as denial; it is a chance to take into account the overall quality of a relationship. It also helps to withhold judgment until we have more information: "I don't have to respond to any of this now. I'm simply going to listen and then find time to plan what I will do."

Attending to our inner dialogues can also be a spiritual practice. Many spiritual traditions suggest the use of short words or phrases as a way to pray throughout the day. They may be called mantras, ejaculations, or affirmations, but all are forms of prayer that help change our self-talk around anger. Such prayer represents ancient spiritual wisdom about the way inner dialogues become distorted. Rhythmically repeated, these prayers refocus attention or bring about inner stillness; they replace negative thinking with more balanced and hopeful words. Synchronized with our breathing, they can help us act from a deeper source.

We can draw such prayers from many sources: favorite hymns, biblical passages, treasured sayings, or names for the Holy. If no prayers of your own occur to you, try breathing in and out with words like: *Wisdom; Spirit; Come, God.* Or use phrases from biblical passages such as Isaiah 43:1–5, which can steady us as we find our way through an angry incident:

> Should you pass through the sea, I will be with you;
> or through rivers, they will not swallow you up.

> Should you walk through fire, you will not be scorched
> and flames will not burn you.

> Do not be afraid, for I am with you.

Because they are short and repetitive, prayers like these can be recited while driving or walking, or in brief intervals between personal encounters. Choosing ones that suit us is a way to name and honor the inner conversion that is part of individual work with anger.

A concrete accompaniment to such short prayers is the use of prayer beads. The form of prayer beads most familiar to us is the rosary, but such beads were in use five hundred years before the birth of Christ, and have been used to support many kinds of prayer and meditation. Prayer beads are earthy, grounding, and can be used to anchor a mantra. Working the beads has the added advantage of giving us something physical to do with our energy. Their use reflects centuries of spiritual insight into the unity of mind and body.

5. Mixed Emotions

I often see visions of poisonous green smoke; I am with the hungry, with the ill-treated and the dying, every day, but I am also with the jasmine and with that piece of sky beyond my window; there is room for everything in a single life.

—Etty Hillesum
An Interrupted Life[1]

I remember a phone call I once got while working in a nursing center. A few weeks earlier I had admitted a woman in her seventies, a former nurse with a long string of nursing honors. Now she was suffering from advanced Alzheimer's disease, and most days did not recognize anyone she had formerly known. A strong, determined woman, she still retained the outward manner of a hospital supervisor, and her family found it excruciating to witness the dimming of her mind. That morning's angry call was from her two sisters, Louise and Mary. I had met them when I admitted her. "We're not happy with Roberta's care," Louise shouted into the phone. "What kind of a place are you running there?" Mary interrupted. "You've already lost her best blouse and pantsuit." They continued in this vein for some time, their voices and accusations escalating. Then there was an abrupt silence. Finally Louise said: "Oh, Kathy. It's just that we're so *sad.*"

No emotion is simply one thing. Each is complex and multifaceted. This is especially true of anger. It seldom appears in a pure state. Rather, it usually rides into town with emotional companions: sadness, fear, shame, guilt, anxiety, caring. Some arrive ahead of it; others follow on its heels. When we say we are angry, we are using that word to cover not simply one feeling, but a mixture of emotions.

37

Anger is internally layered.

Think of anger as the outer layer of an onion. As the anger peels away, we find other feelings. This is why anger has at times been designated a secondary emotion. An underlying feeling frequently tells us *why* we are angry. If we look beneath the anger, we recognize that we are feeling helpless, powerless, frustrated, hurt, discounted, ignored, put down, afraid. Something we value is at stake: our view of ourselves as perfect, the health or happiness of someone we love, our sense of fairness in an interaction, a matter of justice for the poor or homeless.

Since anger maximizes the human capacity for self-protection, it is a useful tool of psychological defense, a convenient cover for inner experiences that threaten us. Being angry momentarily blocks painful feelings such as embarrassment or guilt. It obscures awareness that we are feeling empty or frustrated. Anger temporarily suspends any sense of wrongness or badness in the self, since these interfere with the goal of self-defense.

We are especially prone to use anger as a way to express anxiety or fear. Martha Howard, one of the main characters in Linda Raymond's novel *Rocking the Babies,* muses on her angry outburst: "Did she really believe that? Talking to people was a strain. She found herself taking on extreme views, sounding angry, when what she really felt was fear and the possibility of being misunderstood. She knew her insecurity led her to overstate."[2] Any parent of a teenager can tell you how worry can trigger anger. One mother describes it this way: "Tim had instructions to call if he missed his 1 A.M. curfew. When he had not appeared by five in the morning I was beside myself and had entertained numerous scenes of flaming car crashes. As he walked in the door, I let loose my fury: 'Where have you been? Who do you think you are, walking in so smug like that?' Of course, beneath that fury I knew I was anxious out of my mind. I wanted to hold him and weep because he was home safe."

Watching anger in action reveals other examples of its complexity. We are hurt by a critical review at work, and to avoid hearing what is true in it, we lash out about the poor management in the company. We feel bad about coming late to a luncheon appointment and, instead of apologizing, we rant about the freeway traffic. The difficulty with using anger to block painful experiences is that it prevents us from dealing with the underlying feelings themselves and from addressing the problems that generated them. We miss the chance to face our fears and losses, say what hurts, fill the emptiness. It can take some time to get to this second level of feeling and accurately name what is going on. That is why a period of cooling down and reflection is so helpful before we act on the anger. Then we are better prepared to deal with the real issues.

Contradictory feelings coexist in us.

Not only are feelings layered, they occur in confusing combinations. It is particularly hard to integrate the tough and gentle emotions, to make room in ourselves for both. In the pages of her diary found in *Of Woman Born,* the poet Adrienne Rich records the alternating anger and tenderness she experiences as a mother: "My children cause me the most exquisite suffering of which I have any experience. It is the suffering of ambivalence: the murderous alternation between bitter resentment and raw-edged nerves, and blissful gratification and tenderness." At times, Rich confesses, she feels like a monster, or weak, from held-in rage. At other times, she is filled with a sense of her children's beauty and her love for them. Some years later, in her poem, "Integrity," she describes how such anger and tenderness can breathe in her one self "as angels, not polarities."[3]

Many experiences generate this confusing tangle of anger and love. My friend Marjorie discovered this while caring for her parents. They were elderly and ill. She was trying to get her father to agree to move to a care center. Her mother was in the hospital, ready for the assisted living facility she had selected. Her father was still at home, refusing to budge. Marjorie was at wit's end from trying to convince him that there was no way mother could come back home. She recounted an especially conflicted moment for her. She had gone to get her father to take him to see her mother, feeling furious with him as on all recent visits. When she got to his house, he asked if he could have a moment and then began to weep. He wanted time, he said, to pick some roses from the yard to take to her mother, the kind she especially loved. Looking at his tear-stained and wasted face, Marjorie was suddenly flooded with compassion. Inside, this feeling was at war with her exasperation with him. What was she to do with it all?

We need them both. Rage alone can lead to violence and destruction. Compassion without rage leads us to settle for the status quo. We experience a universe of complex feelings when we make moral decisions.

The psalms let us voice all our conflicting emotions.

The psalms are a school for restoring strong feelings to the spiritual life; they vividly depict the full range of human emotion. A woman whose son was being hospitalized for a drug addiction said her capacity to deal with it was strengthened when she had a rage session with God, using familiar psalms to pour out all that she did not understand and could not accept about the way this world is run.

Like human existence itself, the psalms move back and forth between anguish and comfort, anger and thanksgiving, despair and hope. Moods intermingle even within the same psalm. In Psalm 6:6-8, for example, we find the psalmist weeping one moment and furious the next.

> I am exhausted with my groaning;
> every night I drench my pillow with my tears.
> I have grown old surrounded by my foes.
> Leave me you who do evil.

Psalm 22 moves from despair:

> My God, my God, why have you deserted me? (v.1)

to hope and praise:

> You are the theme of my praise in the Great Assembly....(v. 25)

Biblical scholar Walter Brueggemann suggests that the predominate patterns in the psalms reflect the way life flows from "satisfied seasons of well-being" through "anguished seasons of hurt, alienation, suffering, and death," to "turns of surprise when we are overwhelmed with the new gifts of God."[4]

The psalms do not explain anger, but they give it poetic expression. They are candid about resentment and the desire for revenge.

> I stayed dumb, silent, speechless,
> though the sight of [the wicked] thriving
> made torment increase.
>
> My heart had been smouldering inside me,
> but it flared up at the thought of this
> and the words burst out....(39:2-3)

For years when I read the psalms I censored out the bold and disruptive passages. If a phrase conflicted with what I had learned theologically, I went with the theology. Now, though I still avoid those stanzas that seem too full of the language of ancient warriors, I am grateful to find prayers that are as chaotic and tumultuous as my heart often is, thankful to find words for the feelings that seem too awful to confide to anyone else. For example, I often resolve to rein in my angry responses only to find myself expressing them anyway. At such times, Psalm 39 is my solace:

> I said, "I will watch how I behave,
> and not let my tongue lead me into sin;
> I will keep a muzzle on my mouth
> as long as the wicked one is near me." (v. 1)

Because the psalms provide such a free and full expression of the range of emotions we feel when angry, they can be a very helpful prayer for clarifying and coming to terms with it. Moreover, this kind of honest prayer provides the sense that the Divine is a solid holding-place for our anger.

The psalms are helpful in another way as well. They situate our emotions within a wider company of women. A collection of songs, poems, and prayers used by both individuals and communities in many different social and historical settings, they reassure us that we are not alone in what we feel. Five biblical women—Miriam, Deborah, Hannah, Judith, and Mary—responded to significant events in their lives with psalmlike songs and prayers.[5] Each reflects on a recent reversal in her life or that of her community, and gives thanks for its resolution (Ex 15:20-21, Jgs 5, 1 Sm 2:1-10, Jdt 16:1-17, and Lk 1:47-55). Countless communities of women have made the psalms their own and prayed them daily. This larger communal context not only supports our honest expression of emotion; it witnesses to the eventual resolution of pain and anger.

6. The History of Our Feelings

Neither healing nor liberation of the whole self—body, mind, spirit, and feelings—is possible without memory, a memory that is comprehensive, honest, and discerning.

> —Rita Nakashima Brock
> *Journeys By Heart*[1]

In one of her essays in *Sister Outsider,* the African American poet Audre Lorde tells of an incident when her own past pain rose up as anger at her son, Jonathan. When he was eight years old and in the third grade, they moved to a school where Jonathan's life as the new kid on the block was hellish. Jonathan did not like to fight, to play rough games, to stone dogs. All this marked him early on as an easy target. When he came home crying one afternoon, his sister Beth shared that the corner bullies were making Jonathan wipe their shoes on the way home whenever she wasn't there to fight them off. Lorde says that when she heard that the ringleader was a little boy in Jonathan's class and his own size, her fury at her long-ago impotence and her present pain at his suffering made her forget all she knew about violence, fear, and blaming the victim. She began to hiss at her weeping child: "The next time you come in here crying...." Then she stopped herself in horror. She realized that what was rolling over her was her old fear, the old panic of being the fat kid who ran away, terrified at getting her glasses broken.[2]

We sometimes puzzle at the strength of our anger. It seems out of proportion to a person or event, like a bulldozer when a shovel would do. This disparity is one clue that we are borrowing energy from past experiences. The past can augment present anger through unfinished business or emotional memories. The roots of present angers are often planted deep in the layers of the heart.

Acknowledging them, finding meaning in memory, is an essential aspect of coming to know our angers.

Unfinished Business

Sally, a bright and accomplished woman in her forties, cannot stop weeping as she recounts a blow-up with her husband on the previous weekend. While she was away on a business trip, her husband Jake arranged for the two of them to have dinner with his brother the night she returned. She did not want to see the brother, who was visiting her husband while she was away. When she realized what Jake had done, Sally found herself out of control and furious. "I just lost it," she said. "One part of me knew it was overkill. I realized I had not given Jake all the information he needed about the situation, but I wasn't able to control my response to him."

When I asked Sally if what she felt was familiar in any way, she said it went back to the first year of marriage, when she and Jake lived near his brother and she worked as a clerk in the brother's law office all summer. He was critical and demeaning, and Jake did not defend her. She began making notes to herself about getting a divorce, but never discussed her feelings. "Now," she said, "I hate to go back to it because it feels very painful to do so. I had nowhere to turn. Now it feels like the emotions of a child—but I know I felt powerless, emotionally abused, and enraged. I just stuffed it all."

Recognizing that we have unfinished anger from the past is an important part of integrating anger and love. If the energy we bring to an event seems out of proportion to what is happening, it helps to reflect on how *then* relates to *now*:

What am I feeling?

Is it like anything I have felt before, especially while growing up?

How can I take care of the feelings connected with that earlier event or relationship?

What do I want and need now? What behavior in this situation would be more in keeping with my present beliefs and values?

Do I need help in dealing with the feelings getting triggered by this event?

It may be possible to let past hurts go, or we may need to deal with them more directly before we can move on. In either case acknowledging them separates present anger from the weight of the past. Anger that is freed from past injuries, disappointments, and unacknowledged resentments has more power in interactions and is less easily dismissed by others.

Emotional Memories

If the scent of lilacs or a few bars from a Strauss waltz bring back the feeling of largely forgotten events, you know what emotional memory is.[3] Such memories are the felt residues of past experience, traces of persons, situations, things, or events. A bowl of soup, a song on the radio, a funeral service can produce feelings in us we do not understand. Sometimes they seem almost an echo, a past part of ourselves we cannot quite reach.

We learn to do many things—tie our shoes, drive a car, play the piano, attend church, say familiar prayers—in a particular emotional environment that continues to form the underlying emotional tone of these activities. Our body remembers and it freezes or trembles. We constantly push ourselves to achieve more or punish ourselves when we fail, just as our earliest caregivers did. We expect or dread events. We overreact. Such remembering is largely nonverbal and hard to put into words; we know more than we can say. This is not necessarily bad; it is deeply human. There is always more to our experience than words can express.

As a child, and later in life, we learn about anger from the important relationships in our lives. We watch how problems are settled. We notice the tone of voice and body language used when people are angry. We are present while others use violence, tantrums, intimidation, withdrawal. We are aware of long-standing bitterness when problems are not resolved but pushed under the rug. During the course of a lifetime we have also learned what it feels like to have someone angry at us. To a child, anger is terrifying. Adults are powerful, and children depend on them for every aspect of life. As a result of childhood experiences with anger, we may avoid anger by being compliant, or deny feelings and needs in order to be safe.

In *The Healing Connection: How Women Form Relationships in Therapy and in Life,* Jean Baker Miller and Irene Pierce Stiver provide a helpful term for this aspect of our history. They speak of relational images.[4] These images are the inner models of relationships we each create out of what has happened to us. We begin developing these images early in life, and then elaborate on them and revise them as we move along. Much of the time we are unaware of doing this.

As we are constructing these relational images, we are also forming beliefs about why our relationships are the way they are. These are the meanings we attach to the experience. Like the images, they do not always reflect the total situation accurately. We do not always know why a person cannot respond to us or why they respond in a certain way. We create many of our most basic relational images as children, in the context of our families, at a time when we are not mature enough to understand the complexities of emotions and relationships. We may not know that our parents are dealing with mental illness, marital problems, economic crises, alcoholism. Since children have few explanations for things outside ourselves, we often conclude that there must be something terribly wrong with us for others to treat us the way they do.

If we can let in new relational experiences, these images can change. If not, they become quite fixed. To modify them, we need experiences in which we feel heard and understood, hear and understand others, and feel more worthwhile and capable of action. But frequently it is hard to stay in the pain and fear and sort out the mixture of feelings we find in these relationships. The feelings they evoke can be extremely painful, sometimes too painful to explore without another person who can respond to them. If this is the case, it is important to get help in working with them.

While these images can be deep-seated, they can also heal. This is why mutual relationships are so sacramental. When we are loved or related to in a different way, our relational models shift, and this shift affects all our other relating. In fact, I have been repeatedly struck by the fact that women who emerge from very difficult childhoods with many strengths can point to an important adult who showed them a different image of themselves and of relating. Often this was a teacher, grandparent, or aunt. Sometimes it was the parent of a friend. Often it was a relationship with God that got them through tough times and taught them what it means to be loved and safe. The attraction to prayer first emerges for many women in these early years.

Traumatic Memory

In Toni Morrison's novel *Beloved,* one of her characters, Sethe, speaks of the daily task of "keeping the past at bay."[5] Sometimes an experience is so powerful and painful that it affects all our subsequent days. It is impossible to talk about anger today without looking at the issue of trauma. We are coming to understand the power personal trauma has to shock and wound a person to the core.

A traumatic event is one in which we feel completely helpless in the face of a force we perceive to be life-threatening. The ordinary human responses to danger that prepare the body to fight or flee are of no avail. Judith Herman puts it precisely: "When neither resistance nor escape is possible, the human system of self-defense becomes overwhelmed and disorganized. Each component of the ordinary response to danger, having lost its utility, tends to persist in an altered and exaggerated state long after the actual danger is over."[6]

Survivors of trauma frequently say that they are not the same persons they were before being traumatized. Catastrophic experience can create in us a hostile, mistrustful attitude toward life; a chronic feeling of being threatened; a sense that the world is a dangerous place. Research is beginning to show that these experiences not only alter our sense of self and our relationship with family and community. They change our biochemistry itself. Moments of overwhelming terror can alter brain chemistry for decades. Some of the persistent rage and anger we experience is due to this change. In other words, uncontrollable stress—rape, repeated abuse in childhood, near-death in an auto accident—has a biological impact. Although there is much we still do not understand about the underlying brain chemistry, it appears that repeated adrenaline rushes progressively sensitize brain chemistry, so that there are ever greater floods of adrenaline at lower thresholds.[7]

Childhood rage is the result of violations of body and soul through neglect, abandonment, incest, and sexual or physical abuse. These injuries invalidate a child's autonomy and self-esteem. In the midst of these primary wounds a child comes to believe that her selfhood is unworthy and that she is somehow to blame for her own inadequacy. When her self-worth is threatened in later life, rage rushes in to shield the self. It operates according to the early patterns that she creatively discovered and that enabled her to survive. Now these patterns may prove destructive to self and relationships. To break out of them these hurts need to be acknowledged and mourned, so that a woman no longer has to rehearse the rage endlessly. Because of their intense power we need the safety of professional help in dealing with traumatic memories.

Anger, Spirituality, and Life Story

Life's most powerful experiences can only be known through story. Anger cannot be understood in terms of isolated feelings, thoughts, or incidents, but only in the patterns of a life. Through memory we come to know the story of how we learned to be angry and what we learned to be angry at. What is puzzling and mysterious is no longer so hard to grasp when we see how it fits into this larger story. For some angers, this naming itself makes the difference, enabling us to choose different emotional expressions. Story becomes the crux of change. When we recollect and remember, we are free to repeat or not repeat certain patterns.

Other angers call for deeper healing work. Though some kind of counseling is the usual context for such emotional healing, it is also affected by everything that is happening to us. Life events provoke anger; they also alter it. Grace moves in unexpected ways. A chance meeting, a new friendship, an apology, an illness or death, or the experience of being loved well by someone can be key elements in this process. The death of my own father was such an event for me. It occurred exactly two years ago today, on the fifth of January, 1995. Two long-distance phone calls came from the nursing home in the early hours of the morning, the first to say that his breathing was rapid and his temperature rising, the second to tell me that he had just "passed away."

What I remember most about the memorial service we held later that week is the rain—the relentless downpour that beat on the glass roof of the small church in which my immediate family huddled. I needed this cleansing. I had not expected much from the funeral ritual or the service we prepared for the scattering of his ashes over Puget Sound. But, perhaps because ritual has such power to reach emotional depths, these enabled me to name and understand in new ways the conflicting emotions, especially the anger, I was unable to express when my father was alive. Only with his death did I find the freedom to do that work. In the process I came to know more fully the roots of my anger and the way it has shaped my life narrative.

Part of the healing of memory is finding some positive legacy in the past, a story of survival. This is not the same as saying that the evil that happened to us was a good thing. Suffering is never good in itself. But it is possible to draw from it strength and insight. This is the work of the Spirit, somehow redeeming—if only in small ways—what we experience as a fixed barrier to life and happiness. Knowing that from the pain and loss we were able to bring forth sensitivity, resilience, empathy, compassion, or courage can lessen our despair about the impact of such events. One trauma survivor says that such meaning came for her from a life of caring for and being sustained by others. It is especially her newborn son who is the embodiment of her life's new narrative: "Having him has also enabled me to rebuild my trust in the world around us. He is so trusting that he stands with outstretched arms, wobbling, until he falls, stiff-limbed, forward, backward, certain the universe will catch him. So far, it has, and when I tell myself it always will, the part of me that he's become believes it."[8]

We all need such faith that the universe will catch and hold us, an overarching story of hope to sustain us. We need word of the *Shekinah,* the divine presence that meets us in unexpected ways in a broken world. She is the divine compassion active in tragic situations; her work is that of accompaniment. Wherever the Israelites wandered, Shekinah was with them: in the postslavery wilderness, the years of exile, in all the hostile places and rough times: "Come and see how beloved are the Israelites before God, for whithersoever they journeyed in their captivity the Shekinah journeyed with them."[9] It is this indwelling Spirit we need if we are to find consolation and hope in the midst of memory.

7. Hostility and Community

A tide pool or rock face shows us on a small scale what is harder to see but everywhere present in all other aspects of the planet: unbelievable individuality, diversity, and complexity combined with astonishing networks of interconnectedness and interdependence.
— Sallie McFague
The Body of God[1]

n January of 1997 I was at the beach near San Diego during an especially fierce winter storm. A combination of strong winds, heavy rain, and high tides moved through the area, leaving in its path an ugly, stinking array of garbage on the sand. Piles of ocean-polluting trash had washed up on the shore; tangled with seaweed were plastic toys and containers, soda cans, beer bottles, and beach balls. A lover of oceans since my childhood days on the Pacific Coast in Oregon, I felt heartsick as I witnessed the storm's aftermath, and a nameless rage began to rise in me. I was angry with everyone who was carelessly destroying the world I loved. Then, as I stood at the window stoking my anger with mental indictments of our consumer society, I noticed a young woman gingerly climb the rocks and work her way to the litter on the sand. She proceeded to fill container after container with the debris and haul it away.

In the stress of contemporary life, it is easy to adopt a general attitude of ill will toward others, to walk about with an air of hostility. Though it differs in degree, hostility is an enduring negative attitude toward others. On crowded freeways and in busy grocery checkout lines, people get in our way. We are in a hurry, and they impede our progress. We forget that our lives are wrapped up together. In a world where we are more and more strangers to one another, hostility is one mark of our disconnection.

One current expression of this is road rage, a condition that a few years ago did not even have a name. A University of Washington clinical psychologist and medical school professor,

Roland Maiuro, is one of the world's leading authorities on it. He has found that road-rage sufferers fall into certain groups: the young aggressive male; the Jekyll-and-Hyde profile; the displaced-anger-projected-rage person who has other problems that are not being dealt with; persons who feel urgency, competitiveness, and a quickness to anger; and the rule enforcers, predominantly women, who expect a certain type of etiquette to be practiced on the road and react self-righteously when these rules are breached. But Maiuro really believes that road rage should be dealt with as a public health problem, the result of larger issues such as a failure in public planning, public attitudes and policy, the way roads are designed, the dearth of alternatives to the car, the growing number of weapons in vehicles, and motorists unaccustomed to dire driving conditions.[2] In other words, road rage is a symptom of who we have become and how we are designing our lives. Its victims are the canaries in the coal mine, whose sufferings warn us we have made our world so toxic as to be unlivable.

Moving beyond such rage and hostility is a way of loving both ourselves and our planet. Eliminating it improves our physical health and chances of survival. Since hostility is a pervasive and chronic discontent that affects all our organs, it has proven links to coronary heart disease and premature death. Hostility is hard on the heart. Studies show that it is not so much the isolated angry incident, but the day-in and day-out hostile feelings that put our cardiovascular systems, and our lives, at risk.[3]

Because it concerns the honoring of our deep connections with other people and all of nature, addressing hostility is pivotal to spirituality. We are one body. We breathe the same air and suffocate or thrive in the atmosphere we create. When we notice that a kind of creeping hostility is beginning to fill our days, it is helpful to reflect on several issues that intersect with it.

Anger and Stress

Research shows that anger is closely related to stress.[4] But we do not need specialized studies to tell us that we are more likely to get angry easily when we are under pressure. Stress is a way of

52

describing the demands the environment makes on us. When there is an imbalance between these demands and our ability to manage them, we experience greater stress. It is like a scale in which the weight of our resources is on one side and the conditions of life on the other. We express this by saying that life is weighing us down. When we are ill, tired, or have been trying to handle too much for too long, our ability to cope is weakened.

Though major events can cause stress, it is often the daily hassles that wear us out—misplacing and losing things, problems with coworkers and neighbors, concerns about money or health, a house that needs cleaning. Daily challenges pile up: A car suddenly pulls in front of you on the freeway, and though you manage to avoid hitting it, it goes ten miles below the speed limit and you are unable to pass it. The new refrigerator you ordered arrives with a large dent on one side and you cannot convince the company that it happened during the delivery. Your son brings home a progress report with an F and two Ds after several weeks of assuring you he was doing better in school. Psychological stress tends to be more pronounced in those activities and settings in which we spend the most time and have the strongest commitments. For most people that means work and family.

Often the annoyances of everyday—the key that will not work or the friend who arrives late for lunch—can be dealt with by some combination of humor and perspective. A high level of irritability is often related to time pressures, exhaustion, or even depression. Attending to these areas is a way of taking care of it.

Two spiritual practices also help reduce this kind of stress and anger. The first is a movement toward simplicity. Gospel sayings remind us repeatedly that it is crucial to keep our hearts fastened on what truly matters.

For where your treasure is,
there will your heart be also. (Mt 6:21)

Look at the birds in the sky. They do not sow or reap or gather into barns; yet God feeds them. Are you not worth much more than they are? (Mt 6:26)

Many people are heeding this call by cutting back on material possessions, and the attendant need to work at a crushing pace. This provides a slower life rhythm, time to really attend to family and friends, greater balance and peace.

Some moments of prayerful gratitude also work well. Such prayer offsets the rising frustration and stress that result from a long, hard day. Spend a few moments relaxing and letting your mind wander over the day. Find three good things that happened. They do not have to be large; anything that you can feel grateful for will do: A kind word from a friend. The sunrise on your way to work. Getting a hug from your child. Remember as well the good things you did, what felt satisfying about how you moved through the day. Life is filled with small gifts. Take time at the end of the day to relish some of them and say thank you.

Displaced Anger

When we are angry, the temptation is to vent the frustration on the next person to cross our path. If it is risky to display anger, the expression of it will be disguised. Or it may be displaced, through prejudice and discrimination, on people who pose no threat to us. This is an experience of having the right emotion but the wrong target. Anger that is felt toward one person or event gets redirected at someone or something else. If the anger was evoked by someone more powerful than we are, we may turn it on someone less powerful. Or someone we don't know at all. If our anger and frustration cannot find a direct way out, we move it toward those who will not punish or abandon us. These are often strangers.

Sometimes the wrong person who becomes the target of our anger is ourselves. One of the most costly ways in which women displace their anger is by expressing it at themselves through self-hatred, guilt, feelings of worthlessness, self-punishment, and self-defeating or even self-destructive behaviors. We ourselves become both the victim and victimizer.

When I worked in a bank for a time, I noticed that during the days around Christmas, customers would bring huge amounts of anger to bear on simple issues or mistakes: Someone had not given them a proper receipt, or their statement had arrived a day late. After trying to problem-solve for these people, I began to realize that all the emotions the season evoked for them—all the sorrow, nostalgia, resentment, and hurt—was getting put on this banking problem. It seemed for them the only safe place for it to go.

But the universe is a closed system. All this displacement of anger merely recycles it. Hostility and displaced anger differ from the passion that fuels our work for justice. That emotion propels us to work for the future of the world and its peoples. Generalized negativity and misdirected anger, in contrast, weaken our common bonds. Like toxic waste left to seep into a stream or river, they poison the environment for everyone.

Interrelationship as a Fact of the Universe

One woman who had worked for years on what she termed her "anger problem" found that she needed to learn a whole new way of being in the world. Its basis was kinship rather than alienation from others. She noticed that when she approached all those strangers she met in a day of normal activities with some openness to their humanity, they responded in kind, and she experienced a connection rather than the sense of being besieged.

I have had similar experiences. Recently, as I was looking for the grocery checkout stand with the shortest line, a woman insisted on following me from place to place. Having pursued me to an available checker, she then cut in front of me and set two frozen lemon cream pies on the checkout belt. This time instead of fuming at an apparent affront, I decided to try something different. So I turned to her with a less than wildly creative comment: "You must like lemon pie." "Yes," she said, "I cut each one into thirds and it makes a nice big piece. I throw away the crust; I don't like crust. I eat what and when I like. At ninety-two, you get a little crazy." Somehow my feelings toward her did a complete switch. Here was another human being struggling with some of the same conditions of existence that I do. I left with thoughts of how free I might like to be at ninety-two.

Anger is not a private matter. The welfare of any individual is shaped by forces that extend throughout space and time. We live in an organic universe, an intricately woven web of life. Since nothing exists in isolation, we cannot disturb any element of nature without upsetting the rest. All things are related in the great circle of life. Consider bamboo plants. Once each century, all of a certain kind of bamboo flower on the same day. The plants' location does not matter, whether they are outdoors in Malaysia or in a greenhouse in Minnesota. Nor do their age or size make a difference. They flower: "Some current of an inner language passes among them, through space and separation, in ways we cannot explain in our language. They are all, somehow, one plant, each with a share of communal knowledge."[5]

Emotion and Our Unity with Nature

The energies of the universe move in and out of us. In *Riverwalking*, Kathleen Dean Moore writes about the possibilities of emotion throughout nature. Sometimes, she says, in a desert landscape, she can feel emotion lying on the surface of the sand and seeping through the boulders:

> There is joy in the wind that blows through the spines of the saguaro, and fear in bare rocks. Anger sits waiting under stones. Exhilaration pools in the low places, the dry river beds, the cracked arroyos, and is sucked by low pressure ridges up into storm clouds that blow east toward the Alamo Canyon.[6]

Traveling in India taught me also how the rhythms of life are shaped by the emotions of nature. The monsoons in India are enigmatic and mysterious. They can bring life to a region, but also chaos and destruction. They bless one area with abundant waters and deny another relief from intense heat and drought.

Why be surprised if our emotions are tossed about by the weather? Having grown up in the Northwest, I am used to a substantial number of cloudy, overcast days. When we have a string of unusually bright, sunny ones, something in me feels slightly amiss, as though I am inhabiting an alien landscape. When I first went to California to study for my doctorate, I would relish the comforting sound of rain when it came. If we are as closely bound to the landscape as science tells us, why would it be a surprise that on dark winter mornings it is hard to drag ourselves out of bed to go to work? Or that as the first days of spring arrive, we burst with a new kind of energy? Our salty bodies, like the great oceans, are pulled and held by the gestures of the moon. We are in this way in tune with the environment, but often barely conscious of it.

Our bodies are dynamic energy systems. This energy flows in and out of the rest of the universe. We have not yet fully taken account of the profound interaction that exists between the earth's energy and that of the human body. Since we do not end with our skins, we affect and are affected by all that surrounds us. We cannot deal with our anger, then, unless we see it as related to our diets, landscapes, noise pollution, and all the other factors that affect us each day. Energy fields interact not only within an individual, but also between one person and another, and between one person and the entire cosmos.

Coming to know our angers, then, means living in the universe in a different way. We become conscious and careful of all the forces impinging on us and likewise mindful of the pathways of our own emotional expression. Moreover, we are able to see our angers in light of larger ecological concerns and our commitment to care not only for one another, but for an increasingly endangered planet.

Section II
Integrating Love and Anger

8. Anger and Self-Esteem

The first time I said, "You're wrong" to a great theologian friend of mine, I was shocked at myself; I thought it couldn't be me talking. It was not the first time I had thought differently from him on some aspects of theology, but I had never dared to express my disagreement. I had taken a leap forward in life....I had moved from being an echo to being a voice.

—Elsa Tamez
Las mujeres toman la palabra[1]

ow we view ourselves is a powerful factor in the appraisal that accompanies anger. Our self-image is the lens through which we filter events. If our self-worth is low, it can lead to two different distortions: Either we find offense everywhere and are constantly angry, or we do not notice when we are being treated unjustly and fail to be angry when it is warranted.

The results of recent research illumine this relationship between anger and self-esteem. The first large-scale study of women's anger, completed by a group at the University of Tennessee, found that women with higher self-esteem had fewer physical symptoms in response to anger. They also had less tendency to brood or ruminate over anger incidents, were less likely to vent their anger outwardly in a blaming way, and were slightly less apt to hold anger in.[2]

A woman with a low sense of self may increase her anger and further lower her self-esteem by thinking that the situation proves someone does not like her, that she is powerless in the situation, or that her worth has been attacked. If, in addition, she suppresses her anger and holds it in, there is no chance for her to hear from other sources whether or not her perceptions are valid. She may also keep the anger alive by continuing to replay the event in her mind to the point of obsession. This leads to a vicious cycle of increased anger and lower self-esteem. Keeping anger in prevents communication and problem solving. The person who has been blamed or attacked by the woman may respond by withdrawing love, avoiding her, or counterattacking, confirming her belief that anger is not acceptable.

The development of a strong sense of self is the foundation of work with anger. Emily Dickinson says it with her usual wit.

> I took my Power in my Hand—
> And went against the World—
> 'Twas not so much as David—had —
> But I—was twice as bold—
> I aimed my Pebble—but Myself
> Was all the one that fell—
> Was it Goliath—was too large —
> Or was myself—too small?[3]

There are many reasons why we fail to value ourselves fully, but spirituality has played a large role in teaching us that we are inferior as women. Fresh spiritual resources are addressing this issue at its core, and three areas of this reassessment are especially significant for a consideration of anger.

Believing That We Are Enough

The womanist theologian Toinette M. Eugene reflects on what has enabled black Catholic women to resist the negative images that both church and society have maintained of them. They have, she says, been strengthened by a spirituality of survival. This spirituality embraces at least two aspects: it fosters an empowering of self-esteem and it affirms the presence of God in the day-to-day struggle for justice and survival.[4] Though developed and sustained in a unique way by black women, these same qualities are essential to the spirituality of all women.

Throughout the centuries women have found the roots of self-love in a divine presence at the heart of reality. Contemplation is the crucible that refines our angers. For in it we gradually come to know that we are loved, just as we are, by the Spirit of life who made us. This does not happen all at once, but is a gradual process of opening ourselves again and again to the Divine. We find in the poetry of the thirteenth-century German mystic, Mechthild of Magdeburg, a description of this encounter between self and Self that affirms the unique value of each reality in creation:

> A fish cannot drown in water,
> A bird does not fall in air.
> In the fire of its making,
> Gold doesn't vanish:
> The fire brightens.
>
> Each creature God made
> Must live in its own true nature;
> How could I resist my nature,
> That lives for oneness with God?[5]

This turning toward the Divine is also a turn toward all of creation, human community, and our own deepest truth. Acceptance at this level prepares us to reenter community with a different clarity. In it we find our own voice and authority.

Mechthild's life is witness to such an inviolable, divinely rooted sense of self. A member of the Beguines, an independent community of laywomen who led lives of good works and spiritual practice, she was a bold and witty woman. The Beguines are sometimes credited with beginning the first European women's movement. They were women who refused to relinquish living the kind of life they desired. When in the twelfth century the church refused to open any more convents, women in several northern European countries came together to create their own common life. They were able to thrive in spite of a church atmosphere that became increasingly clerical. At their height, some Beguinages housed thousands of women, and included hospitals, chapels, and cathedrals within their walls. Though attacked as being heretical and hounded by church officials in other ways, Mechthild managed to survive as a Beguine for nearly fifty years.

As Mechthild's life and that of other women of prayer testify, a habit of contemplation frees us from constantly monitoring others as a way of knowing our preferences and desires. We do not depend on them to make us feel worthwhile. Their disapproval does not then devastate us. In other words, in contemplation we find a center that holds.

Since the divine presence permeates all of creation, our biggest challenge is simply to open ourselves to it, to let ourselves be loved by God. Methods of contemplation are meant to help us do that. Whether they show us how to walk through the world with greater awareness or teach us to attend to the Presence within, they gradually shift the lens we bring to all of life. Then, when there is injustice and lack of love, we see it. But we are also ready to let others love us and to believe we are worthy to receive that love.

Healing Our Internal Images

Women frequently tell me that they can think positive self-images in their heads, but these images do not feel true emotionally. Negative images still feel like the deepest truth about themselves. This is because images have most power at the level of the imagination, where body and spirit meet. An image arises from our emotional impressions of a particular event; it is an experience of embodied truth.

Forms of prayer that engage the imagination are needed to shift this sense of self. The truth of the imagination is more symphonic than logical. It does not reach us directly, but approaches from all sides. The use of active imagination in prayer enables us to move beyond intellectual understanding and to experience something with our whole being.[6] This can happen, for example, when we take a scripture passage and hear the word as spoken to us, or enter into one of the parables and relive it from the points of view of the different characters.

We might hear the word of God in a passage addressed to us as reassurance that we do not have to earn divine love:

> Oh, come to the water all you who are thirsty;
> though you have no money, come!
> Buy corn without money, and eat.
> Why spend money on what is not bread,
> your wages on what fails to satisfy?
> Listen, listen to me, and you will have good things to eat

64

and rich food to enjoy.
Pay attention, come to me;
listen, and your soul will live. (Is 55:1-3)

Or we might let our selves become Mary of Magdala as Jesus appears to her after the resurrection (Jn 20:11-18), experiencing ourselves as known and loved personally. Entering into any passage in this way requires that we come to our senses, moving with our imagination into the event and reliving it as if it were our own experience. After quieting and relaxing ourselves, we bring the details of a scene to life by seeing and hearing all its dimensions: the time of day, the mood, the land, the people, the voices. We are no longer an onlooker, but a participant. Such imaginative contemplation moves us beyond intellectual understanding to a kind of felt-knowledge.

Chants are another kind of prayer that does this, especially when they are set to music. Chanting, as those who have done it testify, engages more dimensions of our being than rational understanding. Now, neurological research shows that the pulse of chanting helps integrate the workings of the right and left sides of the brain in processing information.[7]

Nearly all religious traditions, including Buddhist, Hindu, Jewish, and Christian, use some form of chant. Women often create their own chants from stanzas of favorite songs or hymns that they listen to and sing over and over again.

In Native American poetic forms, all ceremony is chanted, drummed, and danced. American Indians often refer to a piece of music as a dance rather than a song since a song without dance is rare. Healing chants and ceremonies emphasize the restoration of wholeness, for disease is seen as a condition of separation from the harmony of the whole. God is the All Spirit, and the natural state of existence is whole. Acknowledgment of this dynamic unity in the circle of being allows healing chants, such as this from the "Night Chant," to heal, or make a person whole again.

Happily I recover.
Happily my interior becomes cool.
Happily I go forth.
My interior feeling cool, may I walk.

No longer sore, may I walk.
As it used to be long ago, may I walk.
Happily, with abundant dark clouds, may I walk.
Happily, with abundant showers, may I walk.
Happily, with abundant plants, may I walk.
Happily, on a trail of pollen, may I walk.
Happily, may I walk.

The repetition integrates. It makes breath, heartbeat, thought, emotion, and word one rhythmic whole.[8]

The reiteration found in many religious chants gives words time to lodge within us and surface at other moments. When we are moving quickly from one idea to another, it is difficult to let any one idea sink in and deepen. Repetition is a kind of doubling back, which slows the movement of prayer and intensifies the experience. Because it allows time for the words to connect with our own experiences and feeling, the pattern reaches not only the mind, but the body and feelings as well.

Honoring Our Desires

According to Iroquois cosmology, there are diseases that result from the resentment of a soul whose desires are not being met. Not the usual conscious desires, but those that dwell deep in our hearts and reveal themselves in dreams. When these desires are denied, the soul revolts against the body. Disease follows. Many sick people identify deep wishes they must fulfill in order to go on living.[9] So, too, spiritual health depends on finding what our soul truly needs for nourishment. This deepest desire is our eros, our erotic energy. Life's passion is one, whether expressed in the love of the divine, human love, or the energy that heightens and strengthens all our experiences.

Some anger results from the fact that we never get around to our own agendas, our own creative pursuits. In *Silences,* Tillie Olsen explores the creative voice that is muzzled: "...the unnatural thwarting of what struggles to come into being, but cannot."[10] Olsen was nearly fifty when she published her first novel, *Tell Me a Riddle.* Throughout the earlier years of her life she was too

66

exhausted from raising four children and supporting them with menial jobs to have any energy for writing.

As women, we learn to repress our basic needs in order to be loved. Spiritually expressed, this becomes a question of what we must do to win God's love. If we must deny our basic desires and surrender ourselves to be pleasing to God, then what is left? This tendency to silence our hungers has been supported by a focus on self-denial as a basic component of spirituality. We can feel slightly righteous when we are fasting or denying ourselves pleasure. And hate ourselves when we eat fudge brownies and ice cream for dessert. On this scale of evaluation, an anorexic woman would be a very good woman, having transcended all the desires of her body through denial. She is not only very good, but perfect. A love-hate relationship with food is a major source of conflict for many of us.

Food is a replacement for emotions: It calms us when we are angry, soothes us when we are upset, comforts us when we are sad. But turning to food will not satisfy our deepest cravings. That we have been taught to fear these yearnings only makes them more inchoate and powerful. They are, rather, guides to our internal knowledge and needs. An emotion such as anger tells us what we value and whether it is in danger. It is an invitation to ask, What do I love? What is it I desire? It is a call to make time for personal pursuits that satisfy us, to make room for the kind of solitude that brings refreshment, to see our hungers as holy.

These, then, are some of the ways in which love of self is intertwined with our angers. Convinced that we are enough, that we are loved, and that we can listen to our hungers, we are better able to recognize and direct our anger in healthy ways. Since it is a lifetime's work to deepen a positive self-image, I have summed up these convictions in the following "Woman's Creed." It is meant to support and strengthen this continuing movement toward a strong sense of self.

I believe that I am created in the divine image, that my body and spirit are holy.
The God who dwells in all of creation lives in the inmost depths of my being.

I believe that I am loved by God just as I am, without conditions or demands that I be more. I am enough. This love sustains me when I am in doubt and upholds me when I fail.

I believe that God desires my freedom and wholeness, the full expression of my talents. I need not live by the values of others, nor silence my self to please them. I can let my own voice ring out, my own song be sung. I can trust what I feel and know, living out of my own deepest truth.

I believe in the power of women to heal and love, to seek truth and justice. This faith is strengthened when I remember the women throughout time who have used their power and gifts to change the world: Sarah, who answered God's call; Esther and Deborah, who saved a nation; Mary Magdalene and the other women, who announced the resurrection in the face of skepticism.

I believe that my gifts and strengths are for cherishing myself, others, and the world. The more I care for myself, the better I will be able to care for all living beings.[11]

9. Good Girls Don't Get Angry

God is not glorified
by half persons.
—Ruth Burrows
Before the Living God[1]

hen Mother Teresa of Calcutta died in 1997, a newspaper account quoted one of her first students in Calcutta's Motijeel slum as saying, "Mother was full of love all the time...even if she was angry, she never showed it." Perhaps that is true. But the comment also illustrates how hard it is for us to imagine anger in a woman already popularly acclaimed a saint. In fact, adjustments to the public image of Mother Teresa began long before her death. An independent Albanian churchwoman, she set out in the 1940s to follow her own vocation from God. She succeeded because she was deterred neither by established institutions nor approved behaviors. Though she was an autonomous, assertive woman, her life is now told primarily as the tale of a compliant daughter of the church. This strong, determined woman has became a symbol of conformity.[2]

Those who control the images of holy women know how important images are. When the ideal woman offered us is a feminine prototype devoid of anger, as in the usual depiction of female saints, we find it hard to embrace and work with our own anger. Much is at stake here. That is why women are beginning to rescue holy women from beneath their polished facades, in the process discovering female saints richly varied in their full personhood. This enables us to hold fast to our full humanity and relinquish the pursuit of an oppressive perfection. I have chosen Mary of Nazareth and Teresa of Avila to illustrate this process. First, I show how their stories are being retold today, and then I examine the implications of such revisioning for women's spirituality.

My sister cleaned out her garage recently and returned several of my high school yearbooks to me. Paging through them I was struck by the strong presence of Mary. Her example was used to instill in us the virtues considered suitable for a graduate of Sacred Heart Academy. In one photo several of us are gathered around her statue. She is draped in layers of long, flowing fabric. We are in prom dresses, jackets covering any strapless styles. The caption reads: "Mary shows us how to dress for prom night." This seemed to indicate that she would not approve of those who doffed the jackets when free of surveillance.

The holy cards I collected of Mary while growing up Catholic reinforced this spiritual ideal. Her eyes are averted, gazing up to heaven or down at her son. The Mary I knew combined two features of the traditional presentation of women saints: obedient submission and idealized purity. But she was also a powerful advocate, someone who could intercede for me with a judging God, a woman who had a place in the highest reaches of holiness. Hers was a mixed legacy. She offered me both a constricted image of femininity and a female presence missing in other realms of Catholic life.

Mary's hold on the imagination is such that women are returning to her in new ways today. In a movement led by Latin American women, she is being reclaimed as prophetic and liberating. María Pilar Aquino describes her as an agent and collaborator with God in bringing about the reign of justice.[3] The Magnificat in Luke 1:46–56 affirms this; it has become a key text for the spiritual journey of Latin American women. Its depiction of God putting the mighty down from their thrones and exalting the humble inspires the struggle for justice and reciprocity.

In Latin American base communities Mary is seen as someone committed to joy and abundance for the poor, a model for women who have begun to take charge of their own destinies. Participants in these communities find that Mary did not live a placid existence; conflict marked her entire life as narrated in the gospels. It begins with her unique pregnancy and giving birth in the midst of the strains of the Roman occupation. Later, Mary did not hesitate to contradict her son, but stood by him when he fell out of favor with the religious and civil authorities of the period.

In these communities, less focus is placed on Mary's individual virtues, and more on her active commitment to a new order. She says yes to the God of life and no to the forces that condemn the majority of human beings to a subhuman existence. This is a radical obedience, not the passive submission of traditional piety.

Others are also finding a new Mary. In her autobiography, *Longing for Darkness*, China Galland describes her search for dark images of female divinity. Raised a strict Roman Catholic, Galland is drawn to the figure of the Virgin Mary but finds her "impossibly good, inhumanly pure."[4] Deeply conscious of her own faults, she experiences despair in the face of such perfection and purity. In her travels Galland at first searches outside the Christian church for dark female images, but she later learns about the many black madonnas within Roman Catholicism, and undertakes pilgrimages to Switzerland, Poland, and the Rio Grande Valley in Texas. In El Salvador Galland discovers a black madonna represented as *Madre de los Desaparecidos,* the Mother of those who disappeared at the hands of death squads. This representation of a powerful Mary contrasts with the one she knew in the tradition: "This is a Mary that we need now, a fierce Mary, a terrific Mary, a fearsome Mary, a protectress who does not allow her children to be hunted, tortured, murdered, and devoured."[5] Rather than someone whose power is derivative, this Mary has real power of her own.

In her study of Our Lady of Guadalupe, Jeanette Rodriguez shows the significance of Mary for contemporary Mexican American women. She is a model of strength, competence, enduring presence, and fresh possibilities. As Yolanda, one of the women interviewed, says: "She may look quiet and calm and everything, but that takes a lot to do. That's why I believe in her the way I do, because I think she's very strong." Our Lady of Guadalupe is someone with whom these women can identify as mother, healer, intercessor, and woman: "I think I have always had her like a torch in my life, a torch that keeps burning, and there is nothing that can turn it off."[6] For these women, Mary is above all someone who has known suffering and is strong.

Teresa of Avila: Following Her Own Voice

Like Mary, other woman saints are being reclaimed. One of these is Teresa of Avila, the sixteenth-century mystic and reformer, who has inspired countless followers. Thousands of pilgrims flock each year to her native town in Avila, Spain, to honor her. Her writings are a guide to spiritual growth for numerous others, especially *The Interior Castle,* in which she describes the soul as a mansion with seven dwelling places. She invites us to move freely about in these rooms without fear. God resides in the innermost space, where we are invited to union with the Divine: "We consider our soul to be like a castle made entirely out of a diamond or of very clear crystal, in which there are many rooms, just as in heaven there are many dwelling places. For in reflecting upon it carefully, Sisters, we realize that the soul of the just person is nothing else but a paradise where the Lord says He finds His delight."[7]

Though she is now widely embraced as a mystical guide, Teresa's life was not free of challenge. The first step toward her canonization took place only thirty-five years after she was interrogated in Seville by the Inquisition, and just seventeen years after theologians had recommended that all her writings be burned. In *The Book of Life,* Teresa tells us that she belonged to a wealthy merchant family in northern Spain who were *conversos,* that is, Jews who had converted to Christianity during a period of religious persecution in Spain. Her mother died when she was a young girl, and throughout her life, Teresa struggled with debilitating physical illnesses. She was also forced to deal with the prevailing views of women as impure and incapable of leading full spiritual lives. In the early years of her life as a Carmelite nun, Teresa felt God's consoling presence. This was followed by an eighteen-year period of spiritual dryness. But she never gave up on her life of prayer. Gradually, as she moved deeper into the experience of God, she was graced with a new, free sense of self.[8]

What is usually not emphasized in accounts of Teresa's canonization is her strong faithfulness to her inner voice, to the leanings that came from her prayer. She was unwilling to suppress her distinctive insights, even when these came into conflict with ordained churchmen of her day. She faced and eluded the Spanish Inquisition. In the confrontations this entailed, she was confident and tenacious, convinced that no theologian or ecclesiastical authority could dispute what she knew from her own experience.[9]

In her extensive study of Teresa's works, *Teresa of Avila and the Rhetoric of Femininity,* Alison Weber shows us a Teresa who is complex and strong-minded, humorous and ironic, consciously political and strategic in her selection of language for different contexts.[10] Weber describes how Teresa appears to concede to the current characteristics of women's weakness, such as timidity, powerlessness, and intellectual inferiority, in order to use these very concessions to ironically defend her own beliefs. For example, she argues that "little" women may receive more spiritual favors from God precisely because they are weak, whereas learned men have less need of these divine consolations: "In the case of a poor little woman like myself, weak and with hardly any fortitude, it seems to me fitting that God lead me with gifts, as He now does, so that I might be able to suffer some trials He has desired me to bear. But servants of God, men of prominence, learning, and high intelligence...when they don't have devotion, they shouldn't weary themselves."[11]

Through such devices Teresa was able to defend the legitimacy of her own spiritual experiences, her disobedience of the educated clergy, her right to "teach" in the Pauline sense and take administrative initiatives, and her unmediated access to the scriptures. Teresa operated in a sordid world, constantly in danger of inquisitorial action. Weber contends that, well aware of the historical forces she was dealing with, Teresa found a way to creatively subvert them. She used linguistic strategies, such as her apparent self-deprecation, as one powerful tool in doing so. She thus emerges as one example of women who have found ways to function as leaders even in cultures where this is strictly forbidden.

As we can see from the reclaimed lives of women such as Mary and Teresa, holiness is not the same as being nice or good in the ordinary sense of these terms. In fact, what is most striking about holy women is their uncompromising dedication to a vision, and the enthusiasm they bring to a cause. Although she is not on the church's calendar of saints, one of my favorite models of passion for the earth and all living things on it is the environmental activist Hazel Wolf. A founding member of the Washington Environmental Council, Hazel's small apartment is festooned with awards and memorabilia from a life devoted to the environment. She has gone through life fearless and focused. This year, as numerous celebrations were being prepared for her one hundredth birthday, one of her colleagues said of her: "She has the ability to say the most objectionable things in the most unobjectionable manner." She herself says that she has managed to live to be one hundred "by chasing around on matters that need attending to."

True spirituality includes all of life's dimensions, not merely what appears initially pleasing. While traveling in India, I found myself confronted continually by depictions of female holiness, as in the goddess Kali, that represented quite another side of woman's reality. Her black, four-armed image is everywhere; she bears a lotus in one hand and a cleaver in another, claiming the terrain of both life and death. In spite of her huge eyes and fierce appearance, Hindu worshipers are clearly at home with her. What, I wondered, would it be like, if our image of holiness were large enough to embrace all of us, including the anger we feel inside? What if we began to image angry women in positive ways, as clear, centered, compelling? Integrating anger with holiness requires conversion of the imagination.

Much of what we believe about holiness is really about religious stereotypes. These stereotypes of femininity dictate that we have only good and loving feelings. This creates a problem, because none of us can go through our daily schedules without experiencing anger. It takes a lot of energy to see ourselves, and have others see us, as only good and loving. In pursuit of an impossible ideal, we may wall off portions of ourselves, all our bad feelings and

74

thoughts. The good we accomplish does not touch this walled-off place, so we feel increasingly bad, like a fraud. Or we may falsely label mistakes and failures as sin, forgetting that they are simply the human way of being in the world.

This leads us to disconnect through various forms of dissociation, separating our minds from our bodies so that we do not know what we are feeling, or dissociating our voice from our thoughts and feelings so that others will not know what we are experiencing. Most women dissociate in some fashion. Such splitting is a failure to integrate aspects of ourselves into a coherent personal history or sense of self. Often this is the result of trying to separate ourselves from those parts of us that we cannot bear to face. They may be too painful to feel. Or we may experience certain emotions as too powerful to handle, or too unacceptable to acknowledge. So we shut them down and withdraw. Parts of us remain split off and inaccessible.

This division, or polarizing, of the self exacts a price. On the surface, a woman may appear caring, compassionate, and cheerful. Her real self may hide and silently burn. Dana Crowley Jack, in *Silencing the Self,* describes this as a core dynamic of female depression.[12] As anger grows, and a woman's needs and desires go unrecognized, her real self grows more and more blurred, hidden beneath an inauthentic mask of goodness. Left unattended, these feelings take on a life of their own. Anne Lamott gets to the point in her usual way: "Perfectionism is the voice of the oppressor, the enemy of the people. It will keep you cramped and insane your whole life...."[13]

Reclaiming the saints of our traditions opens to us new models of wise women. Their expansive holiness reflects the Wisdom of God as described in scripture:

> In Wisdom there is a spirit intelligent and holy, unique in its kind, yet made up of many parts, subtle, free-moving, lucid, clear, invulnerable, loving what is good, eager, unhindered, beneficent, kindly towards humans, steadfast,...age after age she enters into holy souls and makes them God's friends and prophets. (Wis 7:22–23, 27)[14]

Faithfulness to this Spirit takes different forms in each era. But touched by Wisdom, we are led beyond perfection to wholeness. We are freed to use the full range of our powers in response to life. Though often failing, we move in the direction of truth and love. We learn that genuine holiness is always both tough and gentle, fierce and compassionate.

10. Learning How to Create Boundaries

And a woman without borders belongs to anyone.
— Linda Zisquit
Unopened Letters[1]

ot long ago I got a call from a woman I was seeing for spiritual direction. She had gone away for a weekend retreat and was finding it wonderful. The prospect of returning to all the demands of her life seemed daunting, however, and she wanted me to know that she might just get in her car and keep on driving. She is not alone in her fantasy of leaving it all behind. Many women, when faced with yet another request for help, picture themselves packing a suitcase for the next flight to a remote resort.

Beneath this desire to escape is the kind of anger we call resentment, the sense that everyone wants a piece of us and we are already overextended. Resentment is an early-warning system notifying us that our lives are out of balance: Too much is going out and not enough is coming in. It is a signal that we are being depleted. Anger is the way we establish safety. We use anger to fix limits we feel unable to set in any other way. Anger delivers the message: "Don't get too close." "Don't get in my space." "This is where I end, and where you begin." If we can learn to create boundaries, to say enough and no, we will not have to rely on anger to do it for us.

Speaking the language of no is easier if we are clear about the meaning of three realities in women's spirituality: self-sacrifice, empathy, and responsibility for others. All three revolve around a healthy understanding of the relationship between love of self and love of others.

As women, we are taught to see the highest form of love as utterly unmindful of self: Give without counting the cost. Divine love, understood as the perfect example to which human love should conform, is interpreted as containing no element of self-concern. Religious injunctions about the dangers of selfishness reinforce our socialization to selfless giving. For Christians this ideal of selfless love rests on the mistaken view that Jesus was devoid of all self-concern. But clearly Jesus expected to be loved as well as to love. We hear the anger and sorrow in his cry:

> Jerusalem, Jerusalem, you that kill the prophets and stone those who are sent to you! How often have I longed to gather your children, as a hen gathers her chicks under her wings, and you refused! (Mt 23:37)

Trying to become a selfless saint, avoiding all hints of selfishness, we are puzzled by the degree of anger we feel toward others when they do not adequately appreciate the sacrifices we are making for them, or when they seem able to enjoy life in ways we cannot.

When our self-esteem is low, we have special difficulty saying no. We feel unworthy. We have no right to our limits. We are afraid that saying no will mean losing a job or being abandoned by friends. By just going along, we hope to avoid disappointing or angering others. Or we adopt an indirect style of getting needs met: "Don't worry about me," we say. Others are forced to guess what we want, and they usually end up guessing wrong.

Another indirect way of getting needs met is to talk through others. This establishes patterns where people deal with one another *through* someone else, commonly known as triangles. Triangles arise when we handle the anxiety in a relationship by pulling a third party into the picture. For example: I don't feel comfortable asking you to stop calling me so often, so I try to get a mutual friend to do it for me. Or I tell a coworker what my problems are at work, hoping she will pass this on to our boss so that he will take care of it. Triangles lower the emotional intensity in the original relationship, but do not solve the problem. It is best to stay out of them.

The inability to set limits can leave us chronically angry. We feel others are taking advantage of us. We are overrun and overwhelmed. This is illustrated in the account of a woman who is struggling with her relationship with her mother-in-law:

> And I was still so furious with her that I wanted to strangle her. And I felt that I was just swallowing all this anger, and now I had to be all lovey and nice to her.
>
> The only thing we can do is move to California. I find myself saying really bitchy things about Robert's mother in front of Robert, and I'm having a harder and harder time going over there because I am so angry at her all the time. I have to learn to be angry in an appropriate way. Because when I stood up and started to get angry with her and I started to cry, I thought, "This is a real disaster." I have to be able to get firm and angry, you know, and just say, "Enough." I'm still so angry.[2]

As was the case in this woman's experience, intimate relationships can become prisons of limitless demands. We spend our time and energy on people and activities that do not give us satisfaction, ending up with no time for the things that do. Theologian Valerie Saiving said it well some years ago: "A woman can give too much of herself, so that nothing remains of her own uniqueness; she can become merely an emptiness, almost a zero, without value to herself, to her fellow human beings, or, perhaps, to God."[3]

The path out of resentment begins by recognizing that mutual exchange, not mere giving, is the goal of love. We can ask directly for what we need, and expect others to give as well as receive. We can turn the energy of resentment to creating for ourselves experiences of joy, finding ways of enhancing our sense of well-being. This depends on viewing self-realization not as the opposite of love, but as a basic prerequisite of self-giving. When we are called to love those who cannot return our love equally—children, the sick, troubled friends—we are sustained by love from others who can. Above all, we learn to believe that our longing for reciprocal love and care is not selfish, but deeply true to the divine intention for us.

Empathy is a strength that enhances our capacity to love both ourselves and others well. It provides that possibility of genuine understanding and being understood that is at the heart of human connection. Through it we come to see ourselves in the other and receive in turn the affirming echo that tells us we are accepted. Without empathy, no real intimacy is possible.

Though sometimes caricatured as a soft, primitive, and mindless feeling, empathy is actually a complex art that involves both intellect and emotion.[4] It is the ability to momentarily cross over into another's experience, identify temporarily with that person's emotional state, and then return to a separate sense of self. This knowing is always only approximate, since it relies for the most part on remembered emotional states of our own. A friend calls to tell me that she has found a lump in her breast and is going in for a mammogram. I am able to identify with her fear, let her know I understand, but not carry the anxiety as though I were the one awaiting the exam.

Empathizing well requires both a strong self and sensitivity to the differentness and sameness of another person. Since it demands a clear sense of where I end and others begin, it is a skill that calls for good boundaries. If my boundaries are inflexible, I will be unable to try on another person's experience to see how it feels. If my boundaries are too diffuse, the differences between us will be lost. I must be able both to relax and restructure my borders.

Of these two aspects of empathy, women typically have most difficulty in reinstating a sense of self and thinking through the implications of the experience. We also have trouble showing empathy toward ourselves, having self-empathy: "I care for others sometimes like a sheepherder. I watch and notice and pay attention to their distress. It isn't that I'm just totally accepting because sometimes I point out if I think they're off the mark or something, but I put myself in their place and I understand. With myself, though, I used to be like a lion tamer with a bull whip."[5] Empathy for self is hard because the pull of empathy for the other is so strong, and we are conditioned to attend to the needs of others first. We also feel guilty about claiming attention for ourselves, even when it comes from us.

Psychologist Judith Jordan shares a story that illustrates this dilemma. A bright and creative artist whom she sees in counseling reports that when her husband returns home from work, no matter what her own struggles or accomplishments of the day, she finds herself feeling for him in his fatigue, not wanting to bother him with her concerns. Knowing he likes to talk with her about his day, she encourages him to share with her. She later feels angry, however, that he does not do the same for her; she also fears it is because he does not value her work or her feelings. This woman's empathic response to her husband is caring and important, but as an unvarying pattern, she begins to feel her internal state is not valued as much as her husband's. Because she is so tuned in to her husband's affective state, she sometimes does not feel she has a choice *not* to respond. His pain is her pain.[6] Empathy, then, can lead to the other always coming first at the expense of valuing one's own experience.

The solution to such dilemmas is not to stop caring for those we love, but to bring an empathic attitude to bear on ourselves as well as others and then to ask for what we need. In fact, an understanding of the nature of empathy reinforces the importance of self-love. For without a clear and relatively strong set of self-images, even a temporary identification with the images of another becomes threatening. For instance, a woman will sometimes tell me that it frightens her to be in a room full of angry women. She does not want to hear what they have to say. If we have not dealt with our own anger, the expression of anger in another is frightening, and we want to withdraw. The broader the range of feelings we can tolerate in ourselves, the fuller our empathy can be with others. We may have so focused on others' feelings that we do not know our own: "It is especially hard to deal with anger that isn't charitable — toward those who were doing their best, trying hard, like my parents. I guess I can almost see their point of view better than my own." We then end up in an emotional tangle.

Dealing well with anger requires that we have a sense of connectedness to others balanced by a sense of separateness from them. When we learn to establish clear boundaries between ourselves and others, we do not need anger to do it for us. A young lesbian tells me: "I feel like I'm ready to let go of my anger with my partner. Not holding her responsible for me. Not giving her that power and limiting myself in that way. I want to tell her that I can't meet all of her needs, but I can love her." It is possible to have compassion toward others and still retain a strong love of self, to direct the rich skills of empathy toward ourselves as well as others.

Love and Responsibility: Helping by Not Helping

On one of the buses I ride there is a woman in her forties who gets on with a five-year-old daughter and a husband who is in a wheelchair because of a degenerative neurological disease. Once, as her husband was trying to maneuver his wheelchair into position for the bus lift, another passenger shouted at his wife, "Why don't you help him?" She replied through tears and with her fists tightly clenched, "I *am* helping him." She was helping by *not* helping—a very difficult thing to do when you care.

Christian love is not the same as emotional rescuing, though it is easy to confuse the two. We may have learned very early to feel accountable for others' feelings and problems. This makes it hard to know where our responsibilities to others begin and end. How much is enough? An appropriate sense of separateness in both personal and professional relationships gives others room to feel their own pain and solve their own problems.

If we become caretakers of others, doing more than they want and setting our needs aside to do so, we may face a high level of stress and chronic anger. They will not meet our expectations. We cannot solve their problems for them, and we will be constantly frustrated by our inability to do so. As Harriet Lerner emphasizes in *The Dance of Anger,* it is not our responsibility to shape up other people or solve their problems, and it is not in our power to do so. We have learned to overfunction in relationships.[7]

Learning how not to be helpful is an important task. As women, we care deeply about fostering growth in relationships. We do our best to make them work. When things go wrong, we try harder. We work to establish emotional closeness and make emotional contact. What we often need to do is bring our energies back into our own lives. This is not the same as cut-off and hostile distancing. We can feel the difference in ourselves. It is a matter of not working so hard on the relationship, and directing our energies into our own interests. In this way we allow others to get clear about what they really want and need.

The Skills We Need

Learning to use our anger to set clear boundaries does not happen all at once. It is a matter of developing certain skills. The following will help you begin.

1. Say no with confidence and consistency.

Many times a simple no is all that is needed. Or no thanks. At other times we may want to give the person more information. Complete limit setting usually has three basic elements: It acknowledges the other person, states our position, and sets the limit; for example, "I got your message asking me to take you shopping next week. I won't be able to do it then, but I could do it the following week if you still need someone."

2. Remember that it is appropriate for others to ask and for us to say no.

Our initial response when someone makes a request may be to think they have no right to ask it, or they are demanding too much. The anger behind these thoughts likely comes from feeling pressure to do specific things for others. Some people are very demanding. But we will not change their behavior by focusing on how obnoxious it is. Each of us is the one who really knows and understands our own needs. And people's needs inevitably conflict at times. In a later chapter I suggest ways to resolve such conflicts.

3. Avoid the temptation to apologize, explain, and put yourself down.

It is not necessary to get angry, give advice, or fix the situation. Making apologies and giving long explanations often stem from false guilt.

4. Take time to think about your response.

The desire to please and not disappoint someone is usually strongest when we first receive a request. After a time it is less seductive. One helpful strategy is to make a practice of saying, "Let me think about it and get back to you." After a few moments we generally know whether or not saying yes comes from a true willingness to do it or from other pressures.

11. Love and Anger in Intimate Relationships

> Where anger is hidden or goes unattended, masking itself, there the power of love, the power to act, to deepen relation, atrophies and dies.
>
> —Beverly Harrison
> "The Power of Anger in the Work of Love"[1]

have always liked the story in John 11 where Martha and Mary each speak their piece to Jesus. Their brother Lazarus is dying, so they send for Jesus. He is clearly an intimate friend, but he does not drop everything and come to Bethany to heal Lazarus, as we might expect him to do. He takes his time. In fact, he takes far too much time, and arrives only after Lazarus is already dead and has been in the tomb for four days. We can easily imagine Mary and Martha's feelings as Jesus fails to appear: bewilderment, disappointment, hurt, anger. All this compounded by their immense grief.

What is more surprising is that they do not hide their feelings, pretending that everything is OK. When Jesus finally gets there they do not say: "Don't worry about it. We know you must have had more important things to do. We understand that it was God's will that our brother die." No, they give voice to their anger: "Where were you? How could you have let us down so terribly?" They hold Jesus accountable. And Jesus does not try to calm them down, argue that their feelings are really not justified, or defend himself. He listens, and then he weeps in frustration at death's power to destroy human hopes.

It is sometimes a surprise to learn that this kind of direct exchange is closer to the gospel than what we mistakenly name Christian love. Jesus was trying to bring about the same thing we desire: honest, mutual relationships. He was actually very good at

85

distinguishing the genuine from the counterfeit and at naming what he saw.

Anger, like love, is a form of attachment and caring. We seldom get angry with persons, institutions, and events we do not care about. Toward these we often feel indifference. But anger is a common occurrence in close relating. Anger in intimate relationships, especially at one's mate, tops the list of anger provocations ranked by participants in the Women's Anger Study.[2] How can we learn to deal with it well? Sound psychology and spirituality agree on the fundamental features of situating our anger in a context of love.

Anger is essential to growth in relationships.

This contradicts our learned belief that conflict should be avoided at all costs. In following this belief we deny others the chance to learn from us and condemn ourselves to a lifetime of unhappiness. "There is no good time to be angry or have a problem," a woman told me. "You don't want to spoil the dinner, the birthday, the vacation." Anger signals that something is wrong and pushes us to address it and move to something better. When we deny our anger and regularly conceal how we feel, we fail to communicate information that is important to the long-term health of a relationship.[3]

Expressing anger creates a separation—even if it is temporary— between us and another person. This can leave us feeling alone or abandoned, and that is frightening. But even the best relationships go from closeness to breaks to reconnection. The reconnection can move us to a new place. In one study of anger, 76 percent of the targets of someone's anger said they came to realize their own faults because of the other person's anger.[4] Furthermore, the relationship with the angry person was more often strengthened than weakened. When anger is conveyed in clear communication, it is a sign of respect for a loved person. Anger directly and validly expressed in a context of mutuality can be an affirming and bonding experience between two people.

Many of us try to keep our anger in check because we fear the depths of fury that might destroy relationships with those we love most. But long denial can make it more toxic and difficult to handle. If the lid does blow off, it releases anger that has been simmering for a long time and is now ready to boil over.

When Jesus was angry, it was because he believed in mutual, caring relationships. His love was directed toward bringing these about whenever possible. It is not Christian love when we allow another to take advantage of us, abuse us, use us, or ignore us. In other words, Christian love not only allows—but demands—that we listen to our anger and figure out what needs to be done in a relationship. Ethicist Beverly Harrison goes so far as to say that "Christians have come very close to killing love precisely because we have understood anger to be a deadly sin."[5] Emotions and relationships are moving, dynamic processes, not static entities. They need the challenge of anger.

It is not the anger itself, but the way in which it is communicated, that usually causes the problem.

In helpful expressions of anger, we hold the other person in respect in spite of disagreeing with behaviors. Anger and gentleness, anger and positive concern, are not antithetical to each other. When angry, we are usually not feeling positive about a person. But feelings of regard and consideration for the other person are generally temporarily suspended rather than completely dissociated from our expression of anger.[6] When they are totally absent, the expression tends to resemble hatred and usually evokes a defensive reaction from the other person.

In explaining this point, I often suggest to women that in conveying their anger they include the context, or what I call "the surround." Are they telling a person of their anger because they care deeply about a friendship or marriage and want it to continue and to get better? Then let the other person know this at the outset. People can hear our anger more easily if they realize from the beginning that we value them and the relationship. If we simply talk about the anger without any context, a person may not know if we want to have anything more to do with them, if we have ceased to love them entirely, if we are upset about everything in the relationship, if we want a divorce.

Anger that is integrated with love is free of contempt, revenge, and the desire to injure or put the other down.

In *The Shipping News,* novelist E. Annie Proulx has one of her characters musing on the kinds of love:

> Was love then like a bag of assorted sweets passed around from which one might choose more than once? Some might sting the tongue, some invoke night perfume. Some had centers as bitter as gall, some blended honey and poison, some were quickly swallowed. And among the common bull's-eyes and peppermints a few rare ones; one or two with deadly needles at the heart, another that brought calm and gentle pleasure.[7]

Like love, anger comes in many shapes and sizes. Some support and expand love; others undermine and destroy it. Clarity means sorting out the different types. There is a Buddhist teaching which states that there is really no such thing as a fire. Instead, there are only kinds of fires: wood fires, cotton fires, paper fires. We sort out our angers to recognize those that are helpful and those that are destructive both to us and to our relationships.

When the desire for revenge is present, the expression of anger becomes an attack on the other person and elicits fight-back responses. Since our initial feelings of anger carry a strong sense of wanting to get back at a person who has hurt us, it takes spiritual work to move to a place beyond this. This is why we often need time before we are ready to talk.

In his twenty-year study of what makes marriages last, psychologist John Gottman uncovered some helpful insights into how people manage anger in successful long-term relationships. He found that not only is a certain amount of negativity not harmful, it is required for a relationship to thrive. The anger and disagreement that produce temporary misery are healthy in the long run. Facing conflict helps couples deal with those things that will harm the union over time.

But Gottman's other findings are equally important in distinguishing the negative energy that improves from that which devastates a marriage. He discovered that no matter what style of dealing with conflict a couple uses, they must have at least five times as many positive as negative moments together if their marriage is to be stable.[8] The ways in which couples manage to put more weight on this positive side of the relational equation are not complicated: showing interest, being affectionate, indicating that they care, being appreciative, expressing their concern, being empathic, being accepting, joking around, sharing their joy.

Another conclusion Gottman reached was that in spite of a wide range of differences in occupations, lifestyles, and the details of their lives, the long-term couples displayed a remarkable similarity in the tone of their conversations. They maintained a strong undercurrent of love and respect. In contrast, Gottman found that the attitudes that doom a marriage are contempt, criticism, defensiveness, and stonewalling or withdrawing from interaction.[9] He sees contempt, often expressed in small facial gestures like a curled upper lip, a sneer, the rolling of eyes, as the most corrosive of forces in a relationship.

Moving beyond contempt often demands difficult inner work. A woman describes her spiritual struggle as she finds her way through a hurtful episode with a friend. The friend had scheduled a trip to a place that the woman had long wanted to visit, and had invited others—but not her—to come along. "At each step of my process I felt I had a choice to blame and beat on her. I had to fight to stay out of that place."

There are losses and risks involved in letting go of the silence surrounding our anger.

The poet Denise Levertov gives us a portrait, "In Private":

> He silent and angry,
> she silent and afraid, each looking
> out the cab windows,
> he to the left, she to the right,
> both dressed for winter, driving
> somewhere neither wants to go.[10]

We struggle with the decision to open ourselves to another human being. If we try to talk about what is really happening with us, anger becomes an open, exposed state. Anger that is a genuine communication in a relationship conveys our vulnerability and reveals something about ourselves. This often has power to open up new levels of communication, but in the process we put ourselves at risk.

The desire to avoid this vulnerability is one reason we lash out against the other rather than talking about what is going on within us. It is much easier to tell the other person what we dislike about their behavior than to speak of what has been stirred in us: hurt, fear, anxiety. Not too long ago, my husband, Tom, and I were walking near the Pacific Ocean in Cannon Beach, Oregon. It was a starless night and pitch black as we wandered away from the lights on the shore. Tom moved on ahead, paying no attention to where I was. Suddenly I found myself totally alone in complete darkness, unable to distinguish the river near our cabin from the ocean, fearful of losing both my footing and my way, having visions of being swept out to sea. Somehow I stumbled back up to the shore and found again the lights that guided me home. Once we had both made our separate ways back, I exploded in angry accusations about Tom's total disregard for me. Some moments into my tirade I realized that what I really needed to say was how afraid I had been, how alone I felt, how anxious I had become. This was compounded by my anger at myself for not taking control of the hike in the first place and establishing my bearings in the way I would have if I had been on my own. These were the harder things to say, and I covered them with my outburst.

Besides making us vulnerable, honest expression of anger can, in fact, put relationships at risk. Most of the complications regarding anger occur when relationships do not provide well for the expression and reception of anger. When we can express our experiences in a relationship and have them heard, the anger subsides quite quickly. But we cannot determine how another person will respond, even when we have carefully prepared what we will say. Several questions can guide us as we weigh possible approaches:

—*How significant is this relationship in my life? In other words, how much energy and time am I willing to invest in resolving the issues around my anger? Once I open the issue, am I willing to stay with the process to its completion? In important relationships this means a commitment to a dialogue that is prepared for and planned. It is not a hit-or-miss, careless kind of activity.*

—*Is there a reasonable hope of a fair and fruitful exchange? What has been my experience of this person's response to conflict or the discussion of emotional issues? Some relationships can handle a great deal of anger; others may dissolve at the least expression of it. It is not always possible to tell ahead of time which it will be, but some clues are available from past experience. Timing is also important here. A person who is under great stress may not be able to hear us until they get somewhat regenerated.*

—*Am I willing to risk the loss of the relationship if the person is unable to handle my disclosure? There are some relationships we cannot leave. This is the case with a number of the nonmutual relationships we encounter in life and work. If I know, for example, from others' experience that my boss cannot handle any negative feedback, I may have to find ways to deal effectively with my anger outside of work.*

The goal, though it might seem idealistic at times, is a relationship where most of our exchanges are mutually empathic and mutually empowering.

There are differences between women and men that turn up again and again in intimate relating. When I told one of my friends that I was writing a book on women and anger, her first response was to say how frustrated she gets in her marriage by the fact that she can never get angry with her husband because he cannot handle it. When she does, he just walks away, leaving her fuming all the more. "Why can men get angry and we can't?" she wanted to know. One theory is that men and women tend to have divergent emotional styles. Generalizations about these may or may not apply to you, but they tend to be true for many couples.

The first is that women are more comfortable in intimate relationships and more adept at negotiating intense emotions. Men are more easily overwhelmed and flooded by strong emotions: "In a nutshell, boys typically are not taught the skills necessary to navigate through the shifting emotional tides of an intimate relationship while girls are given intense schooling on the subject. Like a person thrown overboard without first being taught how to swim, the average man is understandably fearful of drowning in the same whirlpool of emotions that a woman easily glides through every day."[11] In addition, there is some evidence that men have a stronger physiological reaction to certain emotions such as anger. They are therefore likely to be stonewallers, withdrawing when women introduce emotional material. This is very destructive to a relationship. And it is easy to interpret the silence as rejection, disapproval, or hostility.

Integrating love and anger means that the goal of our anger is not to hurt the other person, but to improve the quality of the relationship. If we do not expect true mutuality in a relationship, we will not work toward it. Here is where the gospel can provide a vision and spiritual energy. In a mutual relationship, both are engaged together in the thoughts and feelings evoked by an event. There is movement. Each person is able to add something more to the conversation as it progresses. Such an exchange has the capacity to enlarge both persons and the relationship itself. It is mutually empowering because both people benefit.

The challenge of such communication is to stay in it and be with the process until it reaches at least a preliminary resolution. When we turn away from another without recognizing their feelings, we are both diminished. Can we learn this kind of empathy? Yes. Mutuality allows something new to happen, allows each person to make a contribution to the dynamic: "Mutual empathy is the great unsung human gift. We are all born with the possibility of engaging in it."[12] It requires not only listening and imagination, but the gospel hope that something new is possible in our human patterns of relating.

12. Receiving Anger

It is unsettling to feel one's own anger, difficult to find effective ways of expressing it, difficult to be the target of another's anger, difficult even to stay in the presence of angry people.

—Carroll Saussy
The Gift of Anger[1]

n *Final Gifts,* their collection of insights into the special needs and communications of the dying, two hospice nurses, Maggie Callanan and Patricia Kelley, tell the story of Liz, a nurse dying of breast cancer at thirty-two. When she was diagnosed, Liz was working in a small hospital in her hometown. After treatment, she returned to spend her last months in the hospital where she had worked. It was a difficult situation. Liz was experiencing a great deal of physical pain. While her coworkers were saddened by her situation, they also found it hard to deal with the steady stream of complaints from an angry Liz.

However, the nurses also noticed a pattern. Several times a week, Liz's coworkers from another unit would bring lunch to her room. They would talk about how things were going on her old unit and discuss patients Liz had known. During lunch, Liz would get grumpy, and the rest of the day she was short and hostile with the nurses on the unit where she was dying. One night a nurse who cared for Liz talked with her about it. She learned that the visits with her coworkers were hard for Liz: "I know this will sound childish and awful," Liz told her, "but they make me mad when they come in here and tell me what's happening on *my* unit. Sooner or later, they go back to work, and take over what I want to be doing. I have to lie here in this stupid hospital and die!"

With Liz's permission, the evening nurse spoke to some of her coworkers, who had frustrations of their own. "Liz didn't used to be like this," one said. "It's very hard to spend any time with her; I

guess I'll come back and see her when she's through being angry."
The evening nurse explained what was happening and suggested
a change in approach. The next day a friend from the old nursing
unit asked Liz what she would like to talk about. Liz mentioned
her love of gospel music, and they spent the visit singing along to
one of her favorite tapes. Another coworker visited later that week
and directly addressed the fact of Liz's illness: "I miss you a lot at
work," she said. "I feel so sad about what's happening to you."
This led to a real discussion of their friendship, their sadness, and
the hope that they would meet in another world. They were able to
weep and hug one another.[2]

Receiving anger is as important a skill as expressing it. In some
ways it is even more challenging. Since we are all just beginning to
know what to do with anger, the anger we receive is not likely to
be any more elegantly constructed than that which we convey.
Listening to another's anger can be like walking on an icy side-
walk in January. It requires that we take one step at a time and
plan our next movements carefully. But if we believe anger has the
power to create better connections, then we need to prepare ourselves to hear it from others.

First, be clear about abuse and violence.

Although I discuss violence against women in another chapter,
I want to emphasize here that ordinary approaches to another's
anger do not apply to anger that is abusive or violent. The first
thing we need to do when someone is angry with us is determine
if we ourselves or someone we love is in immediate danger physi-
cally or emotionally. If we are, direct expression of anger is not
safe. Our energies should go toward getting help. This is especially urgent if drugs, alcohol, or weapons are involved. Further, if
any exchange begins to escalate toward name calling, yelling, or
attacking, we need to call a time-out and remove ourselves from
the situation. Even if we feel guilty, we should not allow ourselves
to be verbally battered. Even if we are wrong, we do not deserve to
be called names, threatened, or violated.

The abusive quality of anger is not necessarily equal to pitch of voice. Someone can be screaming at us but saying: "Can't you hear me? I love you!" And someone can be speaking in a very controlled and quiet voice, yet ripping us to shreds. The abusiveness is measured by the disregard for us as a person, the viciousness of the attack, the direct intent to hurt and destroy us. If we have become accustomed to thinking we deserve such treatment, we may need help in learning to recognize and confront it.

When that is understood, I find the following approaches helpful in dealing with the anger that arises in our daily attempts to relate to others.

Listen without feeling the need to agree or disagree immediately with what the person is saying.

The key to receiving anger lies in being a good listener. It may help to remember that when we ourselves are angry, what we want is to be heard and valued. If we remember this while listening to another's anger, we will try genuinely to understand the feelings being expressed. This means being as nondefensive as possible and focusing on what is being said rather than on what we want to say in reply.

Listening with understanding does not mean we agree. This is true whether the anger is about us, other people, or situations in general. It means we are trying to find out exactly what the other person means. This usually entails entry into a longer process than the moment. Resolving anger is not a "hit-and-run" kind of encounter. It includes hearing the anger, sharing our own response, and doing some of the healing work that hurt and disappointment require. But clarifying the issues is an essential first step.

Some practical ideas help with this listening: Focus on the person's bodily and facial expressions and learn to read them. Heed your own body language and try to avoid expressing disapproval and a closed attitude. A goal to work toward is having your own body language and your response to the other person convey that you are receptive to what they have to say. When we are expressing anger toward a person, we are simultaneously noticing if they are rolling their eyes, breathing impatiently, looking away, or shutting down. These gestures tend to escalate our anger.

From the time we are very small, we all need people who can join with us in the full range of our feelings. We want to understand our feelings, sort them out, by experiencing them with another person. Often this was missing from earlier relationships where our anger was denied, ridiculed, or punished. When we are not heard, we become more and more desperate and our feelings intensify.

Try to hear the concerns beneath the anger.

Anger—the feeling itself, not simply the verbal content—is communicating something. Women often describe these bodily indicators as signs of weakness that interfere with the expression of the emotion: "I didn't do a very good job; my voice and hands started to shake." But they are part of the communication.

Frequently, when a person is angry, what they are trying more or less effectively to say is: "Something is not right here. I'm hurt. I'm worried. I don't know how to get you to listen to me. I think I'm being treated unfairly. I want things to change." It may be hard to hear this message clearly in the anger—especially because people often express the cause of the problem as being *us*.

Not all anger is verbal. Some who are angry give us the silent treatment. Others express rage covertly by never keeping their commitments or by performing inadequately in social life or at work. In the presence of such people, we often feel confused. One part of us experiences the anger, but on the surface it parades as procrastination, dawdling, stubbornness, intentional inefficiency, or forgetfulness: A friend always arrives late for lunch. A relative forgets to send us important information. A daughter cannot seem to get dressed in time and keeps the whole family waiting.

Sometimes a friend who is grieving will become angry with us over inconsequential things. It is helpful to remember that it is not primarily us she is angry with, but the universe that took her loved one. In fact, if we are a trusted and safe friend, we may be more likely to hear her anger by reason of that very fact. An older relative may express anger as disgust and disinterest with all about them. What they are often trying to convey is just how hard it is to live without being able to rely on your body, your mind, your sight, or your hearing the way you once could. There is often fear and a sense of isolation: "Nobody understands." Arguing with the anger does not help. Hearing the pain beneath it does. Responding to the frustration, resentment, and fear underneath it usually allows it to dissipate.

Know when to be silent.

In face of the pain and anger of those who know extreme suffering, we are tempted to produce answers. Learning to live with the silence, to realize what cannot or should not be said, is vital to receiving anger. Worst of all is telling victims that they should forgive, or rushing to defend a good and gracious God from their anger. I have always relished an anecdote regarding Elisabeth Kübler-Ross. She was speaking to a group of hospital chaplains who frequently hear the anguished rage toward God of those who have lost loved ones. When tempted at such times to repeat simple explanations of God's will, Kübler-Ross suggested they ask themselves: "Don't you think God is large enough to handle that anger?" Speech that is spare is called for on such occasions.

Be willing to acknowledge your own need for change without turning this into self-beating and self-hatred.

Just as we have trouble seeing our own anger as integrated with love and care, we may see the anger of another person toward us as a sign that they do not love us. Sometimes this is true. But usually it is exactly the opposite—a sign that the person cares enough about the relationship to deal with the real issues in it. Telling us of their anger is then part of love, a commitment to creating a better connection between us. Often women with anger at the church have said to me: "Don't they know that my anger is the other side of my love? I'm angry because I care so deeply."

Anger directed at us is frightening. It delivers the message that we are bad and wrong. It threatens our self-esteem and worth. We fear that a relationship is in danger. This leaves us feeling immediately threatened. A woman is talking about attempting conversations with her older sister: "Much as I want to be a loving, forgiving person, I also want to be myself. I'm afraid of her anger. I'm afraid I won't be able to protect myself from her judgment, her criticism. I'll end up feeling I'm bad."

Perhaps it is hard to hear another's anger because we would rather not know the truth. It frequently contradicts cherished views of who we are and what we are like. A great deal of energy goes into protecting this self-image, meanwhile justifying our actions and reactions. If we have a lot at stake in an idealized image of ourselves, it requires courage to seek and accept the truth about our strengths and weaknesses.

As with all exchanges around anger, the better we are feeling about ourselves, the less threatening the messages will be. If our spirituality leaves room for failure, limitation, and remorse, we will not cease to value ourselves if someone becomes angry with us. We can continue to love ourselves while recognizing that we have hurt another or have patterns that are destructive to a relationship.

Recognize whose anger it really is that frightens you.

If I grew up in a family where anger was out of control and never resolved, the first signs of anger will take me back to that childhood fear. Just as expressing anger calls for work, so receiving it requires spiritual growth. We may deny another the freedom to be angry in order to preserve ourselves from childhood emotions.

Most of our early experience of anger is within unequal power relationships. We anticipate the same patterns in anger between peers. Anger directed at us from another person creates anxiety, the fear that they will tell us something about ourselves we do not want to hear: that we have failed and done something wrong, or that we're no good as a person. But anger between equals is not about being a bad little girl. It can bring insight and change. The discomfort and pain it causes lead to growth.

Do not internalize anger that belongs someplace else.

When we are the object of displaced anger, we are often left with feelings of confusion. I ride the bus to and from work. In addition to being a means of getting from one place to another, a bus is a microcosm of the universe. One recent morning a young woman got on the bus and sat down next to me. Shortly after she had settled in, we reached my stop and I leaned toward her to say that I was getting off. This is usually a simple signal that the person responds to by standing up and letting the other passenger move past. This time, however, she stared straight ahead and in an icy voice said, "We're not there yet." She refused to move. Finally, I asked again, and she left barely enough room for me to get out and shouted loudly after me, "And you stepped on my foot!"

I left the bus unaccountably shaken by the whole experience, and the emotional effects lingered with me throughout the day. I had never seen the woman on the bus before, and will probably never see her again. But I clearly got a blast of anger that was intended for someone or something else. In such cases, our emotional task is to let go of this energy, so that we do not turn it against others who cross our paths.

Ask for a time-out whenever you need it.

It is easy to feel flooded or overwhelmed when someone is angry with us. Anger evokes strong bodily responses. It may even be this bodily cue that first lets us know someone is angry with us. This is especially true if anger is addressed toward us in indirect or concealed ways. For example, someone may start out by telling us that what they are doing is "for our own good." We feel the anger in that apparently altruistic phrase. Or, they make comments about our clothing, our work, our friends, and we sense the anger that is not direct.

Dealing with another's anger requires connection to what is going on in our bodies. We may feel our stomach, neck, or shoulders tighten. Our heart may begin to beat faster. As with our own anger, our body may be readying itself to defend. We feel attacked and threatened, ready to strike back and refute what is being said.

Or we may find all our inner circuits shutting down one by one in a kind of global numbing out that protects us from hurt.

In addition to the bodily responses, there are the emotional reactions. When another person is angry with us, we are liable to feel a complex mixture of emotions: hurt, anger, fear, indignation. We are caught in an emotional maelstrom. How can we respond well in the midst of such a storm?

Often we cannot. That is why we need time to formulate a reply. When that does not happen naturally, we may need to ask for it. Use a simple statement, like, "I'm feeling too upset to listen to more of this now." Or, "I've heard everything you've said. I need to think about it. I'll get back to you." Then establish some physical distance, and take care of yourself.

These and other approaches to receiving anger do not make it easy. But the anger of another person may be a grace calling us to conversion. Yes, we can hurt others. Yes, we are limited and make mistakes. When we have moved through the immediate hurt and defensiveness after someone's anger, it is important to ask honestly: Is this true? Is this person calling attention to something I need to look at? People who have the courage to tell us that something we are doing is causing problems are actually loving us better than those who remain silent and walk away.

13. Resolving Conflicts

> Go-between God:
> inweave the fabric of our common life,
> that the many-coloured beauty of your love
> may find expression in all our exchanges.
> —Jennifer Wild
> *Celebrating Women*[1]

t was to have been a wonderful family reunion. Two sisters and their families flew in from the Midwest. Adjoining cabins on the Olympic Peninsula had been rented well in advance. There was some anxiety, but a lot of anticipation as everyone arrived for the week together. But before the week was over, one sister and her family had flown home without saying good-bye. A brother-in-law vowed never to do anything like it again. The parents were devastated. What had gone wrong? The sister telling me about it said, "When conflicts arose, we had great love but absolutely no skill."

Differences among individuals are inevitable. Though we might wish life were like a peaceful mountain lake with no ripples to disturb its calm surface, conflict is intrinsic to all relating. And dealing with conflict requires more than love. It includes the hard work of learning and practicing certain skills. They enable us to express our feelings, thoughts, and wishes and to stand up for our rights and limits without violating the rights of others. They ask us to let go of defensiveness, the tendency to assign blame and deny any responsibility. Though their language may at first sound stilted and strained, the basic premises underlying these techniques are now a widely accepted part of good communication and conflict resolution. When conflict has escalated to a major level, a mediator, counselor, or some other nonpartisan third party may be needed. But on a daily basis, the following approaches to differences can help us through many difficult exchanges.[2]

State how the other person's behavior affects you.

Voicing anger spontaneously may let others know we are upset. But lasting change in relationships and the world requires dialogue about the sources of anger. This means learning to speak for and about ourselves. In fact, taking responsibility for our own experience gives us power.

No one talks in "I" statements all the time, but they are particularly important when dealing with anger. Because anger evokes a sense of being under attack, we are immediately tempted to attack in return, launching into a series of "you" statements. The urge to blame, accuse, and criticize can feel very powerful. However, this usually evokes more of the same in the other person and simply escalates the conflict. This is where the work of love takes place. Can we get through that hard, other-blaming place and instead use language that describes ourselves? One widely used formula for learning to do this involves the following:

Statement I: The Triggering Event
Statement II: Your Feeling(s)
Statement III: The Reason

Example: Your mother calls you repeatedly at work.

You say:
- "Mother, when you call me at work (I),
- I feel nervous (II),
- because we are not supposed to take personal calls there" (III).

Example: Your son returns your car without gas.

You say:
- "When I got into the car this morning, it was out of gas (I).
- When that happens I feel angry and frustrated (II),
- because I know I will be late for work if I have to stop to get some" (III).

Example: Your neighbor turns her dog loose in your flower beds.

You say:
- "When you let your dog trample my flowers (I),
- I get upset (II),
- because I worked so hard to plant them" (III).

First you analyze and say what happened ("When you do this" or "When this happens"). Then describe this in behavioral terms, for instance, "When you leave the milk cartons on the kitchen sink...." "When you stop work before your section of the report is completed...." Next, share your feelings about what happened: "...I feel irritated." "...I get anxious." "...I become frustrated." Finally, give the reason for your feelings: "...because I can't stand coming home to a dirty house." "...because I end up working late to take up the slack."

The key to the success of this method is that you are direct, clear, and nonattacking. For that reason, it is important that you:

*Describe the triggering event as clearly and concretely as possible. State it in specific terms, stay in the present, and deal with only one area at a time. One reason we get stuck while trying to resolve a conflict is that we throw other complaints and issues into the mix. This makes it impossible to solve anything. It may help to write the single issue that you are dealing with on a piece of paper and put it in front of you.

*Describe your own feelings without saying "You made me feel...." Sometimes we think we are using an "I" statement when we are really using "you": "I think you are being stubborn." Remember that the goal is to describe behavior, not the other person.

*Avoid blaming language such as, "You made me..." or "You should have..." "You make me feel so stupid." "You should have known I would trip over that football." Present the facts without judgment. When most of our sentences begin with "you," it is an indication that we are looking to the other person as the source of the problem and expecting them to be the solution as well.

*Avoid name calling, put-downs, and guessing the intentions of the other person, for example, "You're such a bore—you just never want me to have any fun." If the discussion escalates to yelling, name calling, or unacceptable behavior, it is time to take a break and resume the conversation later.

Make a specific request.

Once we have described another person's behavior and its effect on us, the next step is to make a specific request: "What I think I need (want, would like) in this situation is...." Make your request specific and behavioral, such as, "I want you to spend every Saturday morning with the kids so I can take a class." "I want a staff meeting once a month, but you can pick the dates."

This step in the exchange requires that you know exactly what it is you want. Resolving conflict requires the ability to stand up for ourselves and speak the truth. We do not simply give in because conflict is unpleasant. When we do this, we lose both ourselves and the integrity of the relationship. This ability to believe in and love ourselves also makes it easier to listen to another's truth without finding it threatening.

Listen to the other person without interrupting.

This is difficult, but try hard to do it. Be an active listener. Use a timer and take turns talking. This will help each person really listen for a time. After each person speaks, it helps to take time to tell the other person what you heard. When you can agree about what was said, you are already quite a bit closer to agreement.

We listen to one another to experience each other's perspectives. This is difficult because we often hear our own perceptions when we listen. It is a great spiritual discipline to hear another person's point of view. This step also affirms that each person's needs are legitimate and important. It may require that we accept responsibility for our own role in the problem.

Negotiate a solution.

The key attitude for successful conflict resolution is problem solving. Our aim is not to get the other person to feel bad or to prove them wrong. Rather, we are trying to fix what is wrong. If there is a conflict of needs, negotiation allows us to find a middle ground where we can both get something of what we want.

It helps to look for the mutual benefit area, that is, the zone of agreement conflicted parties share.[3] In any conflict, the conflicted area is always much smaller than the unconflicted. But emotion and tension heighten the disagreement and create a disproportionate focus on the differences. In fact, research indicates that generally we have 15 percent that is conflicted and 85 percent that we already agree on. The way to success is to talk about the non-conflicted aspects first. This helps us both realize how much we have in common and how much we stand to lose.

Then we need to come up with alternate solutions, as many as we can think up, even if they seem silly. It may help to take some time to think and come back with these. A solution should be a compromise, not a situation where one loses and one wins. Rather it should take into consideration what the other person needs or wants. That means both of us will be making some accommodations.

Imagining can help. Picture a workable resolution to the situation that is producing anger in you: How would you feel empowered? What have you done in the past that worked well? Then make a proposal. Or, if the other person does not accept your proposal, encourage him or her to come up with a different solution. Make an effort to engage the other person in the problem solving: "What would you propose to solve this problem?"

This movement back and forth may go on for a time, depending on how complex the issue is. But at some point agree on a solution and give it a try. If no proposal works, or the other person fails to cooperate in the problem solving, you will need to find other ways to take care of your own needs: "If there is no way you can be here on Saturday mornings, I will find a babysitter who can stay with the kids during that time." "If we cannot find a time to attend this play together, I plan to ask a friend to go with me." "Since we cannot solve this issue by ourselves, I will be asking our supervisor to meet with us."

Finally, it is important to know how to exit a conflict situation when it is time, before it gets out of hand. Use approaches that lower the anger energy: appreciation, acknowledgment of areas of agreement, humor, changing the topic, agreeing to return to it at a later date. In working with differences, we are not only resolving immediate conflict; we are seeking long-term solutions that will help prevent future conflict.

Work at resolving the conflicts within yourself that so often get projected out onto others.

When we have not dealt well with our own inner conflicts about our sexuality, our competence, our prejudices, or our failures, we are apt to put these on others. We meet our unresolved selves in the other and try to label, eliminate, or demonize them. Protecting ourselves against the things we fear leads us to categories of *them* and *us:* They are wrong, we are right. They are insensitive, we are thoughtful. They are unreasonable, we are clear.

Difference need not necessarily lead to conflict. It is the urge for sameness that makes it so. Often this is fueled by difficulty accepting the unacceptable in ourselves. When all the unwanted aspects of our selves are owned, they are less likely to be projected onto others. In this way, we see how self-acceptance translates into acceptance of others.

One helpful attitude for the practical work of conflict resolution is a sense of self not built on opposition to others. Western ways of relating often require that we retain our identity through opposition to others. We define ourselves by comparison and contrast. We are more or less beautiful, talented, holy, rich, or famous than others. This is a pyramid model of feeling good. Difference then demands that there be winners and losers. In order for someone to be up, someone else must be down. When we are in the down position, we experience injury to our sense of self. We are angry. We seek compensation. We want to get even.

This one up, one down model of dealing with the differences among us flows from an antiquated worldview, one in which we live over against one another. We now know the world is different from that. We exist in interdependence. The loss of anyone diminishes us all. The gifts of anyone enrich us all. In this model differences exist as potential enhancement.

The idea that conflict is healthy may sound hard to take if we have learned that conflict is a bad thing or that it can never be resolved. We may need to learn that it is by reconciling our differences that we grow in relationship. Differences are inevitable. So is conflict. But it is the path to greater understanding. It is also how we become more loving people.

In his book, *Touching Peace,* the Vietnamese Buddhist monk, Thich Nhat Hanh, describes what is known as a Peace Treaty, a mindfulness practice for processing anger in Buddhist communities.[4] Though not all of its elements translate into other settings, they can stimulate creative thinking about many kinds of conflict resolution. Here is what each of the parties in an angry conflict is asked to do:

I, the one who is angry, agree to:

1. Refrain from saying or doing anything that might cause further damage or escalate the anger.

2. Not suppress my anger.

3. Practice breathing and taking refuge in the island of myself.

4. Calmly, within twenty-four hours, tell the one who has made me angry about my anger and suffering, either verbally or by delivering a Peace Note.

5. Ask for an appointment for later in the week (e.g., Friday evening) to discuss this matter more thoroughly, either verbally or by a Peace Note.

6. Not say: "I am not angry. It's OK. I am not suffering. There is nothing to be angry about, at least not enough to make me angry."

7. Practice breathing and looking deeply into my daily life—while sitting, lying down, standing, and walking—in order to see:

    a. the ways I myself have been unskillful at times.

    b. how I have hurt the other person because of my own pattern of dealing with emotions.

    c. how the strong seed of anger in me is the primary cause of my anger.

    d. how the other person's suffering, which waters the seed of my anger, is the secondary cause.

    e. how the other person is only seeking relief from his or her own suffering.

    f. that as long as the other person suffers, I cannot be truly happy.

8. Apologize immediately, without waiting until the Friday evening, as soon as I realize my unskillfulness and lack of mindfulness.

9. Postpone the Friday meeting if I do not feel calm enough to meet with the other person.

I, the one who has made the other angry, agree to:

1. Respect the other person's feelings, not ridicule him or her, and allow enough time for him or her to calm down.

2. Not press for an immediate discussion.

3. Confirm the other person's request for a meeting, either verbally or by note, and assure him or her that I will be there.

4. Practice breathing and taking refuge in the island of myself to see how:

    a. I have seeds of unkindness and anger as well as the capacity to make the other person unhappy.

    b. I have mistakenly thought that making the other person suffer would relieve my own suffering.

    c. by making him or her suffer, I make myself suffer.

5. Apologize as soon as I realize my unskillfulness and lack of mindfulness, without making any attempt to justify myself and without waiting until the Friday meeting.

As this Peace Treaty shows, conflict handled well leads to new understandings of both ourselves and others. It defines differences from the perspective of our shared humanity, rather than from divisions of *us* and *them*.

Resolving conflict is a process that will include difficult conversations, uncomfortable silences, a reluctance to examine ourselves. It will meet resistance in ourselves and others. It takes time and practice. Just to avoid blaming is an accomplishment. So is real listening. But staying in the struggle translates all our generalities about love and relationships into the specific moments of this particular exchange. It is a crucible of growth, a place of grace.

14. Loss, Illness, and Anger

Sorrow, like darkness, like rain,
blurs all borders and everything comes flooding in....
— Neile Grahman
"The Limits Undone"[1]

newspaper report describes a mother's testimony in the penalty phase of the Oklahoma City bombing. The account tells how Kathleen Treanor, who lost her four-year-old daughter in the blast, takes the witness stand in the late afternoon and calmly tells the jurors that her daughter, Ashley Eckles, was "the sunshine of my life." She says that on the day of the bombing Ashley begged her to stay home and play with her, but she said she couldn't because she had just started a new job. By the time she took Ashley to her in-laws, who watched her during the day, she had settled down: "She threw her arms around me and kissed me one last time, and the next time I saw her was in a box."

At this point, the account says, Treanor's voice got higher and she began to shout. She rose slightly out of her chair and pounded on the lectern as she spoke, looking first at the stunned jury and then at defendant Terry Nichols, who appeared slightly taken aback: "I buried a little white box," she said. "I never saw her again and I had to live with the guilt, the guilt of being a mother who had to work....I wanted to die." By the time she spoke of how her daughter was taken from her and her family, Treanor was crying.

The defense attorney started to rise from his chair to object, but sat back down without comment. However, U.S. District Judge Richard Matsch later told the jury that Treanor, who had also lost two in-laws in the blast, was out of control and may have been try-ing to influence their decision: "The woman lost it, and the vol-ume with which she expressed her anger is something that may have been intended to suggest more to you than she was asked. You'll have to disregard it. Obviously that was inappropriate."[2]

This account evokes many responses. But one is this: How could we not believe that emotional truth is as trenchant as any other kind? Or fail to see anger as appropriate in the face of such loss? Loss destroys what we love and value, calling all aspects of our identity into question. We are under siege, struggling to find a way to go on living. Anger is the appropriate emotion for such a threat to the self. It enables us to cry out against the senseless evil and suffering in the world. At the same time, we know that we must somehow move through the anger if we are not to be consumed by bitterness. This is the spiritual alchemy of grief, the transmuting of anger into wisdom. It begins with acknowledging the legitimate place of anger in loss and illness.

Anger and Grief

Anger is always some part of dealing with significant losses.[3] A woman told me that after the phone call telling her of her brother's death, she walked for hours howling and screaming at the sky. Anger may be the way grief first manifests itself, protecting us for a time from the sadness and fear connected with the loss. Or it may come later, after the weeping. Anger is even more intense when the death is the result of murder or suicide, or when it is sudden and unexpected. It is also strong at the death of children, or when the loss is accidental, painful, or leaves us powerless in other ways. The sense of unfairness makes these kinds of anger very difficult to channel elsewhere.

Anger attempts to assign responsibility for the loss. Often we do not know who to blame for what has been taken. We may search frantically for what we ourselves did or failed to do, or look outside for the culprit. We may rage at God, be furious with doctors and nurses, blame family members and friends, or resent those who have not had to go through the kind of loss we are experiencing. The fault is sometimes placed on the entire system of faith we embraced. It has let us down, failed to live up to its promise. As one woman put it, after being diagnosed with multiple sclerosis: "I kept all the rules, did my best, and now this. What good did it do? I've been a fool to believe it all."

It is not uncommon to feel anger at the very person who dies for abandoning us. In her poem, "No," Jane Kenyon describes such emotion.

> The last prayer had been said,
> and it was time to turn away
> from the casket, poised on its silver
> scaffolding over the open hole
> that smelled like a harrowed field.
>
> And then I heard a noise that seemed
> not to be human. It was more like wind
> among leafless trees, or cattle lowing
> in a distant barn. I paused with one
> hand on the roof of the car,
>
> while the sound rose in pitch, then
> cohered into language: *No, don't do this
> to me! No, no...!* And each of us
> stood where we were, unsure
> whether to stay, or leave her there.[4]

Society squirms when we blame someone who has died for dying, for leaving us alone to cope, for all the things they did or did not do when they were alive. We shun emotions in ourselves or others that threaten our equilibrium; anger at a time of sorrow is unsettling to bystanders. Better the soft tones of sadness; these we can accept and comfort.

The failure to work through to resolution the anger that accompanies loss often leads to bitterness. Bitterness is unprocessed and distilled anger. We become hardened and brittle. Easily hurt. Unhappy and cynical. Feeling betrayed. Adrift without a belief system that can sustain our grief. Perhaps at no other time is the role of a trusted listener of such importance as when our grief finds expression in anger. Grief is a natural healing process, and if we are allowed to move with it, we will survive. A person or community who knows how to hear our strong emotions without judgment, who offers us a refuge in the midst of the unbearable, makes possible a safe passage through these waters.

Divorce and the Ending of Relationship

Many women find it especially hard to move through the anger that follows a divorce. No matter how the relationship ends, there is grief and loss. Judith Wallerstein, a California psychologist who has studied a group of divorced couples and their children for over a decade, has found that both women and men have persistent, intense anger toward their former spouses even ten years or more after their divorces took place. In fact, this never-ending fury characterized half the women and fully a third of the men in her research group. This long-term anger can be highly destructive.[5]

Such rage will not subside if we simply continue rehearsing the pain in the same way. In *Anger: The Misunderstood Emotion,* Carol Tavris laments that anger is often prolonged because our culture offers no rituals of resolution, no way for a community to help its members manage anger as it helps them manage sorrow. She describes a ritual one woman created for herself to help her do this. On what would have been her thirtieth wedding anniversary, she bought two Waterford goblets and some bread and wine she knew her husband liked. She sent it all to him with a note wishing him a happy celebration of his new life. The woman then took a boat trip with a friend, threw roses into the water and officially said good-bye. After she returned home, she burned all her cards with her married name, and put away her wedding dress and photos. She says she felt a lot better when it was over. And she felt good about the way she had treated her former husband.[6]

A woman in spiritual direction once told me about a similar ritual she developed for herself. She returned to the church where she had been married, and in the sanctuary she remembered the good times and the hard times from the marriage. She gave thanks and wept. Then she took off her wedding ring and put on a new one she had bought for herself, one that signified the end of what had been and the beginning of the new life she was going to create for herself.

When we are ill or in chronic pain, we lose a sense of our own power. Kat Duff says it well in *The Alchemy of Illness:* "The continued trials and losses of chronic illness, like all adversities, strip away our margins for error and eliminate the easygoing trust, tolerance, and generosity of well-being. We get fussy, rigid, and particular about our ways and needs, beg for help while resisting intervention, complain bitterly, and take offense readily, in our wounded vulnerability."[7] The process of surgery and recovery, for example, takes us through shock, grief, and rage before moving us on to recovery.

I find it particularly challenging to deal well with the anger and irritability that accompany chronic pain. During some months of dealing with back pain I found myself wanting to scream at people for the slightest infractions. It sometimes took a great deal of restraint not to do so. Periodically my efforts gave way. One evening my husband, Tom, was helping me water our plants because I was not supposed to lift things. Unfamiliar with the way our large Norfolk Island Pine needed to drain, he carried it back to its place too soon, leaving a trail of water on the carpet. At that point all my frustration with not being able to do the things I had previously been able to do, as well as my fear that I would never do them again, came bursting forth and fixed on those stains. I knew even at the time that the anger was really not about how Tom had failed to do the right thing by that plant, but I could not stop myself from weeping and shouting.

Like my own fit about the carpet, our angers while ill can seem petty and unnecessary, both to ourselves and others. We are frustrated when we cannot sleep; angry when we cannot walk, lift, or use our hands as we could before; envious of those who can do what we are forbidden. Anger can also be a symptom of some kinds of illness. One of these is depression. Increased rage, anger, and irritability is one of the indicators that we may be suffering from depression. Seeking treatment for the depression, through therapy and perhaps medication, can lower the level of anger we are struggling to handle.

After the death of a loved one or the experience of illness and pain, we must carve out a new sense of self that incorporates this loss. Our beliefs about ourselves and the world are like the shifting sands beneath ocean waves as they roll out to sea, threatening to take us with them. Two tasks are part of recovering a solid place to stand in such times.

The first is getting clear about who is the enemy. In other words, who is to blame for our loss. The enemy is often not who we think. It is frequently the personal and social conditions that drive a person to despair. Working with families dealing with a sick member, I frequently remind them: You are making one another the enemy. The real enemy is this disease process, the cancer, the Alzheimer's disease, the stroke. It is this senseless stripping of the person we love that is to be battled, not one another or the sick person.

Feelings of anger generally subside as we are able to build meaning out of loss. Rachel Remen, who has lived for more than forty years with a chronic, progressive intestinal illness called Crohn's disease, says in *Kitchen Table Wisdom* that she first reacted to it with rage. When she initially became very ill, she had to consult her illness on the simplest matters: Could she eat a piece of cheese? Sit through the movies without needing to leave because of agonizing stomach pains? She hated the well people and the side of her family that had passed her these genes. She hated her body. This rage lasted for nearly ten years. Things changed shortly before her final year of medical training. Offered the opportunity to be senior resident at a fine training hospital, she could see no way she would be able to handle it and felt the familiar rage at another lost dream. But then she saw at last the connection between her rage and her vitality: "In that first moment of surprise, I had a glimpse of something fundamental about who I am; that at the core of things I have an intense love of life, a wish to participate fully in life, and to help others to do the same." Her rage was her will to live, but it was trapped in its present form, like the power of a damned river. The anger had helped her survive and resist her disease, but in the form of anger it could not help her now to build the kind of life she wanted. She began to see that her pain was nobody's fault, and this freed her to ask for help and turn to others in a way not possible before.[8]

This search for meaning extends to the role of God in illness. In perhaps no other area does the experience of anger connect so personally with what we believe about God's relationship to suffering and pain. One of the added agonies of grief is that God may not appear to be anywhere around. We see this in the poignant case of Jesus alone on the cross, crying out, "My God, My God, why have you deserted me?" His anguished scream contains the strands of pain, reproach, and loneliness we know well. Or, as one woman shouted on the beach in the midst of her loss, "Goddess, do you care? How could you, when I'm just one small dot in your vast universe?"

Hard as it may be to believe when we are walking the path of pain, God cherishes all that we have loved and lost and is with us in the darkness. The death, the illness, the loss of a relationship are not sent as punishment or test. Nor is God an indifferent spectator to our suffering. The outcry against it comes first from God who is deeply involved in the struggle against evil, laboring with us to birth a new heaven and new earth.

> For a long time I have held my peace,
> I have kept still and restrained myself;
> now I will cry out like a woman in labor,
> I will gasp and pant. (Is 42:14, NRSV)

We find here an image of God as a woman angry at what harms and destroys life. There are also other passages that depict divine grief and mourning over the pain of the world. For example, God suffers at the outbreak of war: "Therefore I weep with the weeping of Jazer for the vine of Sibmah; I drench you with my tears, O Heshbon and Elealeh; for upon your fruit and your harvest the battle shout has fallen" (Is 16:9). Knowing that God grieves with us can console us in our sorrow. More than that, it sustains our efforts to hope and resist, to believe that our grief can somehow be transformed. Anger recedes as we find ways to integrate the loss and learn to love again.

Section III
Transfiguring
Anger's Fire

15. Power, Powerlessness, and Working for Change

A truly beautifying discovery for me was to find so much love in anger. It was a fist-up, death-defying love that challenged the unfair conditions of life and muscled in on injustice as it nursed both sides of a nation.

— Barbara Summers
I Dream a World[1]

*I*n *Refuge: An Unnatural History of Family and Place*, Terry Tempest Williams recounts her conversation with a friend visiting from Oregon. Williams is the naturalist-in-residence at the Utah Museum of Natural History in Salt Lake City, and the two are on their way to the Bear River Migratory Bird Refuge. At one point in their drive, her friend asks, "Do you feel rage?" Williams does not answer for some time. Then she replies: "I feel sadness. I feel powerless at times. But I'm not certain what rage really means." Several miles later, Williams asks her friend, "Do you?" "Yes," she replies. "Perhaps your generation, one behind mine, is a step removed from the pain."

As they reach the Refuge, they begin watching for birds, and Williams tells her friend about the burrowing owl's mound she first discovered with her grandmother in 1960. Generations of owls have been raised there, and she and her grandmother have gone back every year since to pay their respects. As they reach the spot, Williams notices that the mound is gone. Erased. In its place, fifty feet back, stands a cinder-block building with a sign, *Canadian Goose Gun Club*. A new fence has been built, crushing the grass. On it is posted a handwritten note: *Keep Out*. The two get out of the car and walk to where the mound has been as long as Williams can remember. It is gone.

Then a blue pickup pulls up alongside them. "Howdy." The occupants tip their baseball caps. "What y'all lookin' for?" The women say nothing. "We didn't kill 'em. Those boys from the highway department came and graveled the place. Two bits they did it. I mean, you gotta admit those ground owls are messy little bastards. They'll shit all over hell if ya let 'em. And try and sleep with 'em hollering at ya all night long. They had to go. Anyway, we got bets with the county they'll pop up someplace around here next year."

The three men in the front seat look up at Williams and her friend, tip their caps again, and drive off. Williams says: "Restraint is the steel partition between a rational mind and a violent one. I knew rage. It was fire in my stomach with no place to go."[2]

Williams's account shows why rage and powerlessness are so intricately linked. Others violate us and what we love, and we feel helpless to do anything about it. We have no way of influencing them or the situation. Or, it is not safe to do so. Feelings rise and, trapped, roil within us. What results is a violent, intense kind of anger, truly like a steaming, lidded pot about to boil over.

Not only rage, but all kinds of anger are tightly interwoven with power. Power is the capacity to influence others and bring about change. It enables us to create movement in interpersonal relationships as well as in the larger social or religious arenas. In situations of equal power this influence flows back and forth in mutual ways. But many aspects of our lives are marked by power inequality. The powerlessness that results both gives rise to anger and makes its expression complicated and difficult. In their study of the subject entitled *Emotion and Gender,* the authors assert that the anger that arises from a sense of powerlessness takes on characteristics of its own; it becomes an ongoing passion, involving frustration of a more long-lasting kind. Further, it has an out-of-control, ineffective quality, since it is a response to strong judgments about unfairness and injustice that remain unresolved[3]

In fact, powerlessness is one of the most frequent triggers for women's anger. Participants in the Woman's Anger Study, done by researchers at the University of Tennessee, identified three main catalysts for their anger: powerlessness, injustice, and the irresponsibility of others who fail to live up to their commitments. Of these, powerlessness is the most frequent trigger. Fully two-thirds of the anger-producing situations mentioned by the women in the study were variations on this theme. These included both anger at themselves for failing to live up to their own expectations, and anger at their lack of power in dealing with others.[4] No discussion of anger can bypass an analysis of power and our response to it.

Anger and the Dynamics of Power

We live in a world where the prevailing pattern of power is that of the pyramid. This pattern characterizes not only our relationships in society and church, but those of human beings to the earth itself. Power is in the hands of a dominant individual or group, those at the top of the pyramid. Others are ranked below in a graded series of subordinations reaching down to the least powerful who form a large base. In every country in the world, women, especially women of color, are part of this base.

In any relationship where one individual or group is dominant and another is subordinate, the dominant group tends to act in certain typical ways. This is true whether the power inequality flows from gender, race, class, or other considerations. The individual or group in power: (1) tends to act destructively to subordinate groups; (2) restricts the subordinate group's range of action, even reactions to this destructive treatment; (3) discourages the subordinates' full and free expression of their experience; (4) characterizes subordinates falsely; and (5) describes all this as the way it should be, usually as ordered and ordained by higher and better powers, ranging from biology to God.[5]

Since anger seeks to right the wrongs in relationships and move them toward greater mutuality and justice, it is always a threat to systems of dominance. In such systems it is suppressed and punished. It is simply not safe or politically expedient for us as women to express our anger directly in many of the contexts in which we live and work. We may be dependent on the dominant persons economically, socially, and politically. Further, growing up at the bottom of the pyramid affects our imaginations in such a way that we take in and believe the images and ideas the dominant group has of us. We internalize a sense of powerlessness. This leads to low self-esteem, passivity, and a view of ourselves as inadequate.

Portraying angry women as unfeminine or out of control serves to undermine our value and preserve the status quo. Carol Kavanagh, who did research on feminist women's survival in the institutional church in Canada, writes: "A number of pastoral associates said to me, 'If only they [the hierarchy] knew what we were really thinking; but women never feel safe enough to share their thinking. They are fearful of being seen as silly, as "overreacting," as "making waves"; they are afraid of being ostracized, being labeled "that angry woman" or, at worst, of losing their jobs. An acquaintance of mine, an ordained minister in a Christian denomination, said that she felt like "lint on the fringe of the garment." " "[6]

No dominant group wants anger in its subordinates. So anger and criticism are suppressed in a number of ways. There may be the threat of physical violence lurking in the background. Or social and economic deprivation. Or the labeling of anger as bad and sinful. Those in power may shame, humiliate, or judge anger, making it appear that we have no cause for it. If we feel it, there must be something wrong with us. Depending on the specific arena, women's anger has been labeled a sign of sickness, emotional hysteria, sinfulness, or lack of femininity.

Living in these oppressive conditions, we are at risk for embracing several beliefs about our anger: (1) We are weak. Anger is suppressed immediately out of fear of retaliation; (2) We are unworthy. Anger is avoided because it threatens to deepen this sense of self-denigration; (3) We have no right or cause to be angry. If the way the world is organized is right and proper, anger against it leads to a greater sense of irrationality and worthlessness.[7]

In *Memories of God*, theologian Roberta Bondi talks about the struggle she experienced as a woman in a university setting. The problem, she says, was that she angered many people just by being who she was: "Even worse, however, was that I could not simply know that the people who scorned me were wrong. I was deeply divided against myself. Part of me was as enraged over my supposed female inferiority as I had ever been as a child, but at least as large a part of me believed, and continued to repeat to my heart, every negative thing I had ever heard about being female."[8]

The expression of anger in relationships of inequality is difficult and complex. It may even be dangerous. It is in such relationships and cultural contexts that our anger gets stuck, distorted, silenced, exaggerated—and feels ultimately self-defeating. What can we do?

Strategies in the Face of Powerlessness

1. Coming Together

Relationships are a source of power and perspective for women. These connections function as a network of friends or colleagues who use their knowledge and influence to help one another. They provide an ongoing context for building a new image of themselves, confronting blocks to creativity, processing anger, or strategizing actions. To meet these needs, women's groups of every kind have mushroomed during recent decades.

In *Defecting in Place: Women Claiming Responsibility for Their Own Spiritual Lives,* the authors examine how small groups enable women to take charge of their own spiritual lives. In these settings women experience their own rituals and alternative liturgies. Many are still affiliated with the church and belong to a parish or congregation. Many are active participants and leaders in their local church. In interviewing Catholic and Protestant women for the study, the authors found similarities in concerns about gender inclusiveness in language and in leadership. But there were also differences in the degree to which the groups felt alienated. After completing a number of in-depth telephone interviews with Catholic women, one of the staff said: "There is a much stronger and consistent anger, and I might even say rage, that comes through about the lack of recognition and inclusion and about the abuse that women in the Catholic Church experience." Catholic women seem to be more intensely angry more of the time.[9]

Theologian Maria Riley speaks of a dominant patriarchal culture and an alternative women's culture that is emerging at the margins.[10] We live in two churches. The one is slowly transforming the other in the Spirit. "Defecting in place" is a metaphor which, as the authors explain, means both to stay and to leave. It means leaving the old way of relating and thinking, being present in a whole new way. Small groups are crucial to this experience.

Echoing this assessment of the situation, Rosemary Ruether encourages women to "move in and occupy any space for ministry that is opened to them and seek to make it livable space." To do this we need to insist on decent working conditions, humanly and legally, and work toward reasonable contracts and remuneration, as well as shared decision making. But Ruether cautions us to keep our eyes wide open to the spiritual dangers of oppressive working conditions. They are hazardous to our health: "So one should not put one's whole life and soul into such communities, but also create alternative free communities of spiritual nurture and support. Both of these options need to exist side by side, if we are to survive spiritually and help the institutional church to reform." The challenge is to bring institutional and free communities into interaction so that they can enliven each other.[11]

By such an approach we acknowledge several hard truths. Oppressive power relations are never going to completely disappear from any institution. Further, the capacity for such unjust relations resides in us as well as in others. We are all in a process of conversion. By refusing to disappear we will not bring about perfection, but we will perhaps create communities where love and prophetic witness are more fully glimpsed.

Coming together in groups also allows women to experience and refine another kind of power, one that is neither power-over nor powerlessness. We are searching for a language to describe this power that differs from control and domination, one that is closer to love. It is the power found in mutual connection where we both give and receive, change and are changed. It operates by persuasion rather than fear and demand. Such power frees the gifts in all participants and empowers them for action.[12]

2. *Refusing to Be Defined by the Powerful*

Naming reality is a very powerful act. It determines how things will be seen and what will be allowed to come into being. Nowhere is this more crucial than in our spiritual lives. The core issue where gender and spirituality are concerned is the naming of God. The symbols we use for God are the center of deep and powerful ideas, feelings, and associations, both conscious and unconscious. These symbols affect a woman's identity and sense of self-esteem from the time she is very young, long before she realizes what is happening. When we do not see the divine imaged in ways with which we can identify, we cannot see the sacredness of ourselves. We are never enough, because the symbols that shape our spirituality are always *other* than what we are.

That is why women are developing new living metaphors, new rituals, new blessings. They are drawing on their own experience as well as scriptural and historical resources to create fresh prayer forms. Communal prayer both shapes and expresses our deepest emotions. The rituals shared in women's small groups are designed to celebrate and nurture their faith experience. They also give birth to a new vision of church and community. The following ritual of blessing is an example of the kind of prayer that emphasizes women's power and courage, while at the same time acknowledging its interdependent nature[13]:

> The women gather in a circle. The shape of the space emphasizes the collaborative power of blessing and is quite unlike the familiar hierarchical arrangement where one person faces all the others. The women connect with each other by touching through the palms of their hands. Since our hands enable us to love, play, and work, the gesture not only calls to mind the importance of this part of our body but also the interdependence of these aspects of our lives. It also makes one more aware of the warmth, power, and uniqueness of the persons whom one touches. One *feels* the energy that links them. There is a moment of silence when each person can experience the power of this gesture. The words of the blessing punctuate the silence. Five women, spaced throughout the circle, read the invocation to which all respond:

Leader: Let us affirm the goodness in each other, the integrity and beauty of our bodies, the insights of our minds.

All: We stand together.

Leader: Let us acknowledge the pain in each other, the strain of struggle, the sorrow of defeat and death.

All: We stand together.

Leader: Let us uphold the daring in each other: the boldness of spirit, the resoluteness of action.

All: We stand together.

Leader: Let us esteem laughter and joy in each other; the irony of circumstances, the delight of relationships.

All: We stand together.

Leader: Let us go forth empowered from this space and time knowing that as we bless each other so we are blessed in God and with God and by God.

All: We stand together.

Some current rituals have the added power of linking us with other women of the past who shared our struggle. Elsa Gidlow, whose birthday was at the winter solstice, gathered friends every year to light her winter solstice fire with a log from the previous solstice's fire. She writes: "I started when I acquired my first own hearth in 1941. I kept the residue of that first fire and have lighted the solstice fires thereafter each year from the previous year's charcoal. I like the feeling of continuity, not only with the years of my own life but with all past women."[14]

3. Acting to Change the System

Anger that is focused provides energy for change. Translated into action on behalf of what we believe in and value, it strengthens

126

and clarifies. Psychotherapist Teresa Bernardez summarizes very well the characteristics of anger that liberates: (1) It is a conscious response to our awareness of injustice and loss, and a break from the injunction to keep silent about them. (2) It involves self-love and awareness of the responsibility of making choices. It is not focused on making others suffer, but on stopping our own suffering. (3) It connects us with our past, enabling us to recover painful memories, grieve our losses, and reconstruct the future.[15]

Sometimes we can work directly to bring about change in a system. But often such direct action is not possible or effective. As Harriet Lerner points out in *The Dance of Anger,* we cannot change others who do not want to change. What we can do is change our own contributions to a system. Lerner shows how relationships are akin to circular dances. As in a dance, the behavior of each partner maintains the behavior of the other. When we relinquish our determination to get others to change, we can shift our efforts to what lies within our power: changing our own actions in the system. This inevitably brings about some change; if we change our steps in the dance, others cannot continue with the dance exactly as before.[16]

The system's model is very helpful in unequal relationships, because it forces us to be clear about what we want and need, and then to take steps to bring it about. Lerner reminds us of two other maxims that apply to this kind of change. Few things are as difficult and anxiety arousing as moving to a new level of assertion and separateness in important relationships. And changing our position will provoke a change-back injunction from others and may make the relationship harder than ever. It would be naive to think that those in power both in intimate relationships and in larger systems are going to rejoice when we change. If we choose to be clear about the self, we need to know that the course will not be easy.

Justice has always come about through faith, hard work, and the persistence of small groups of people. In *Dwellings: A Spiritual History of the Living World,* Linda Hogan says that in 1986 she heard Betty Williams, a Nobel Peace Prize laureate from Northern Ireland, lecture. Williams described how one afternoon she had witnessed the bombing death of Irish children. A little girl died in her arms. An explosion had severed the girl's legs and blown them across the street from where Williams held her bleeding body. Williams returned home in shock and despair, but later that night as the shock wore off, the full impact of what she had seen jolted her. She went outside, screaming out in the middle of the night. She knocked on doors that might easily have opened with weapons pointed at her face, and cried out: "What kind of people have we become that we allow children to be killed on our streets?" Within four hours, the city was awake and sixteen thousand people had signed petitions for peace.

Williams's talk was interrupted at this point, Hogan says, by a man who called out, "You're sick." Undisturbed by the heckler, Williams continued to describe how she had toured the world as a peacemaker.[17]

When We Are the Ones in Power

We are not always the powerless; sometimes we are the ones at the top of the power pyramid. This may be because of our race or class. But certain roles also place us in powerful positions over others as parents, teachers, therapists, supervisors, physicians. We need to take this inequality into account and reflect carefully on the effects of our interactions. Those in subordinate positions are influenced by the threats of bodily harm, force, loss of love, abandonment, or loss of job that is implicit or explicit in any anger we might express.

Situations of power also offer us the opportunity to use the kind of power many women value most, that which leads to the empowerment of others. Power and powerlessness are intrinsic dimensions of the many caregiving situations that are a part of women's lives. So is anger. The person being cared for may become demanding or withdrawn, be demeaning or depressed. Both the caregiver and the person being cared for struggle to deal with anger, feeling helpless and inadequate when they cannot keep from showing it. Moreover, the care provider often cannot leave the person alone, and so has little space in which to process her anger. When I went home to be with my parents after my father had a stroke, I found that there was no room for my emotions. I cleaned the entire kitchen, including the refrigerator and stove, inside and out more than once in those weeks.

The kind of anger that fuels justice may not fit well with caregiving. The rage that powers us to write poetry that will change the world, fight against injustice, or prove that we can succeed when skeptics doubt us, may be much too large for the task when we are asked to perform small acts of nurturance. A friend caring for her mother with Alzheimer's disease finds herself screaming at her at times. So many frightening realities are bearing down on her that containing her emotions seems almost impossible. She does so by taking one day, one hour, even one minute at a time. She has learned to pray. She now knows how complex the integration of power and love in intimate relationships can be. Her mother is experiencing countless diminishments, losses that disconnect words from concepts and feelings, that scramble night and day and the faces of relatives and strangers. This endless dying of the mother she knew evokes rage. But gentleness is what she wants to bring to her daily acts of care.

A Different Kind of World

Power may seem like an unacceptable topic for spiritual concern. But ultimately what we are about is building a world based on mutual relationships. And confronting the powers that prevent this, the barriers of race, class, culture, and gender, was a major preoccupation of Jesus. Structures of unequal power threaten all that we love on the planet, all its peoples and creatures, its very existence. Changing them calls each of us to a thorough conversion.

It also means finding ways to retain hope, the creative expectation that relationships on every level can be different. As disappointments and defeats come, we risk losing this vision. We are tempted to despair. Anger turns to apathy, and we simply do not care any more. *Apatheia* in Greek means nonsuffering; we struggle against its underlying acceptance of powerlessness.

For the courage to stay with the vision, we rely on the community of women throughout the world. Working to release their power, even in simple ways, they are a major untapped resource for hope. At the opening ceremony of the tenth-year celebration of the Global Fund for Women, their efforts were named:

Like wind, women around the world give wings to freedom.

Like earth, women around the world anchor the roots that grow deep and sustain the strength of generations.

Like water, women around the world ensure life, nourishment and healing for the global community.

Like fire, women around the world ignite change and bring passion to all their efforts.[18]

16. Ending Violence against Women

Women ablaze with righteous anger offer an excellent image of
God's indignant power of wrath kindled by injustice.
—Elizabeth A. Johnson
She Who Is[1]

ecently I read about St. Anne's convent in Madras, India,
where the nuns are learning karate. The lessons were begun
after several sisters were threatened or harassed while doing
social work in nearby villages. A nun was murdered in the southern state of Kerala the year before, and another was raped in the
northern state of Utter Pradesh. Several convents were also targets
of break-ins and robberies during which nuns were beaten. One
of the karate students, Sister Yanmitho, puts the training in context: "We will forgive, and we are not violent. But these days, if I
am attacked, I cannot turn the other cheek. I am ready to defend
myself, although I will still pray for my attackers."[2]

Violence against women is a major health and spiritual issue
throughout the world. The possibility of violence influences
where we walk and vacation, what jobs we choose and what hours
we will work, how we regard strangers we meet on the street.
Many of us have ourselves experienced verbal intimidation,
assault, rape, emotional or physical abuse, and battering, or have
seen it in the lives of friends and relatives. Vivid media images
deliver into our living rooms global violence against women: a
twenty-three-year-old peasant woman leaps off a balcony in
Beijing to escape prostitution; women are raped as acts of war in
South Africa, Rwanda, and Bosnia.

The statistics have been repeated so often that their effect is
numbing: Every fourth woman we meet has been raped or beaten
or has experienced incest. Nearly one in every three adult women
experiences at least one physical assault by a partner during

adulthood. An estimated four million American women experience a serious assault by an intimate partner during an average twelve-month period.[3] According to the platform of the Fourth United Nations World Conference on Women held in Beijing in 1995, family violence is epidemic in most societies around the world. It is clear that one of the most dangerous places for a woman is her own home.

Given the scope of violence against women, how can we not be angry? Anger is the natural response to the violation and danger, and it is an essential resource in our personal and political resistance. It is the backbone of healing, moving us from self-doubt and blame to a clear recognition of the wrongs inflicted on us. It is the indispensable outrage that energizes our work for justice. Such anger moves us to action that will ensure that all women are safe.

Yet the spiritual messages we receive frequently inhibit legitimate anger and protest: Wives should obey their husbands. Suffering is God's will. We should forgive those who hurt us. Women are the source of sin in the world. Such religious teachings make it hard to insist on what is true: that abuse is neither deserved nor divinely sanctioned. In order to resist violence ourselves and be present to the spiritual questions of other women, we need to be clear about the meaning of sinfulness, obedience, suffering, and forgiveness.

The Story of Eve and Women as Source of Sin

It may seem strange to link the brief account of the creation of Adam and Eve in Genesis 2-3 to widespread violence against women. But it is a myth that helps define our culture. Studies show that what we learn about gender roles, that is, our expectations of what it is to be male or female, plays an important role in violent behavior.[4] Violence-free families encourage members to choose their own behaviors without the shackles of traditional expectations for their gender. One of the risk factors for violence in men is a rigid belief that they are superior to women and entitled to control their family members, convictions central to patriarchy. Neil S. Jacobson, one of the authors of the recent study,

When Men Batter Women: New Insights into Ending Abusive Relationships, states it strongly: "I'm absolutely convinced that if we didn't have a legacy of patriarchy, there wouldn't be domestic violence."[5] He bases his view on over a decade of research and countless interviews. In a patriarchal worldview, men are to be dominant, active, and in charge; women should be submissive, passive, and dependent. Violence is the behavior used to intimidate others and exert this control. It establishes clear power relations. Female submission is then equated with consent.

Patriarchy is founded on the conviction that this system of dominance and subordination was ordained by God as the order of creation. Stopping violence against women therefore requires reconsideration of the question, "Who is Eve?" From religious pulpits and in media images she emerges as the woman created as man's helpmate (Gn 2:18–23). She is the one who disobeys and eats the apple; she is untrustworthy, gullible, the source of sin in the world (Gn 3:6). A male God creates man first and woman last; first means superior and last means inferior. All these messages make Genesis a legitimating myth for violence against women.[6]

But this standard account, especially as it functions mythically to sanction female subordination and male violence against women, is not supported by a careful reading of the Genesis story in its original context. With her rereading of the creation account, Hebrew scripture scholar Phyllis Trible helps to transform the worldview that permeates patriarchal theology. Her translation and reinterpretation of Genesis 2-3 turns the usual reading of the Adam and Eve story upside down, replacing patterns of dominance and subordination with models of mutuality.[7]

In her exegesis Trible shows that the intention of the account is to show woman and man as equals. The poet of Genesis 2 uses earthy language to depict God as shaping woman from man's rib, just as God earlier formed man from the dust of the earth. But woman is not derived from man any more than man, the earth creature, is derived from the earth. Life, for both, originates from God. The dust of the earth and the rib of man are in each case simply the raw materials for God's creative action. Superiority, strength, aggressiveness, dominance, and power do not characterize man in Genesis 2.

133

By contrast, he is formed from dirt; his life hangs by a breath, which he does not control; and he himself remains silent and passive while the Deity plans and interprets his existence.

Further, the Hebrew word that has been traditionally translated as "helpmate," suggesting an assistant, subordinate, or inferior carries no such connotations. The term means a companion corresponding to oneself. In the passage, what God wants for the man is a companion who is neither subordinate nor superior, but one who alleviates loneliness. The contrast is between wholeness and isolation. The words "bone of my bone and flesh of my flesh" indicate unity, solidarity, mutuality, and equality. Being different does not mean being subordinate.

As for the fact that Eve was created last, if the point of the story were to establish superiority, this would underscore her importance as the culmination of creation. In Genesis 1 human beings are created last to show that they are the fullness of God's creative activity; it is on the sixth and final day that God makes humankind. So also does the Genesis 2–3 account move to its climax, not its decline, in the creation of Eve.

Nor does the biblical narrative sustain a view of woman as weaker or lacking in judgment; in no way does it disparage her. It depicts Eve as curious and perceptive, a seeker of knowledge. It is Adam who is utterly passive. The Indian poet, Kabita Sinha, puts a new twist on the story in her poem "Ishwarke Eve" (Eve Speaks to God):

> I was never
> a puppet
> to dance
> to your tune
> like
> meek Adam.[8]

In seizing the apple, woman is fully aware and acts with decisiveness and initiative. She is clearly spokesperson for the human couple. But the story does not say that she tempted Adam. Nor is he described as reluctant or hesitant. He simply follows her lead, without question or comment. His transgression, "and he ate," climaxes the deed for "the two who are one." The sexes are interrelated and interdependent; they are mutually responsible for their actions. A renewed vision of Eve affirms the intelligence and powers of women. But it does so in a story that places patriarchal culture under judgment. By telling us that we are creatures of equality and mutuality, it opens for us the possibility of a return to that kind of relating. We understand the message of Genesis when, rather than asking what the story is about, we let the myth challenge what we are about.

Obedience and Submission as Womanly Virtues

Women in abusive relationships face a number of complex and potentially dangerous situations. They wonder: Is it safe or practical to resist? Will it endanger my children or myself? Can I resist at a time and place when there will be others to support me? Will they prevent the violence? Am I endangering others by asking them to help me? The difficulty of these and other decisions means that the best thing a woman can do for herself or others in such situations is to seek professional support. This can come from a twenty-four-hour, toll-free women's crisis hotline available in most cities, or at a shelter for abused women.

In addition, one of the most important things all of us as women can do in the face of the potential violence that is part of our lives is to become empowered. This means claiming authority over our own bodies and selves, valuing our bodily integrity, health, and well-being. We need to see our bodies as centers of divine power and grace. Survivor therapy for women who have experienced violence and abuse is built on this commitment to the development of self-esteem and self-efficacy. Its aim is to help a woman find safety and heal from the effects of the trauma, validate her experience and explore her options, restore clear thinking and judgment, and find hope for a future.

Religion not only contributes to violence in the first place, but undermines women's efforts to survive and heal when it holds up female submission and obedience as the norm. Healing requires more than individual efforts; it calls for a change in religious images of docile feminine bodies and subservient feminine selves.

It may seem harmless to include in wedding ceremonies readings from Ephesians 5:22–33, in which wives are told they are to be subject to their husbands in all things. But this passage ultimately reinforces a pattern of inequality in marriage and is problematic for women attempting to free themselves from situations of domestic violence. Like Colossians 3:18–25 and 1 Peter 2:18–20, this text incorporates an ancient household code.[9] Based on the Roman imperial model of patriarchy, these codes give power over the family to heads of families and describe the corresponding duties of wives, children, and slaves. The Ephesian version focuses on the relationship between husband and wife and compares it to the relationship between Christ and the church. This Christianizing of the code creates a tension between the gospel ideals of equality and mutual love and the prescribed order of the patriarchal household. In Ephesians, believers are told to be subject to *one another*. Husbands are exhorted to "love your wives as Christ loved the church and gave himself up for her." For this reason, the message of this section of Ephesians has sometimes been called "love patriarchalism" or "mutual submission." This mixture of the egalitarian and the patriarchal probably mirrors a tension in both the surrounding culture and earliest Christianity. Finally, however, the husband is "the head of his wife," and the overall import of the Ephesians text has been to promote a subordinate role for women in marriage.

Identification of sin with rebellion, and repentance with obedience also narrows our understanding of the meaning and manifestations of sin in our midst. Although their original intention may have been quite different, many scripture passages foster meekness, forbearance, and forgiveness.

> As God's chosen ones, holy and beloved, clothe yourselves with compassion, kindness, humility, meekness, and patience. Bear with one another and, if anyone has a complaint against another, forgive each other; just as the Lord has forgiven you, so you also must forgive. (Col 3:12–13 NRSV; see also Rom 12:9–18, Mt 5:1–10.)

This list of virtues to be practiced by those baptized in Christ is personified in female form. However, such an approach of choosing to suffer with others and waiting patiently for what is to come is possible only to those who start from a position of advantage and therefore have some options.[10] For others, the message is that those who resist domestic violence or sexual abuse are failing in their Christian calling. Such interpretations become major blocks to changing violent situations.

In her study, *Creative Disobedience,* the German theologian, Dorothee Sölle, probes the meaning of Christian obedience. The willingness to act sacrificially is deadly and destructive, she believes, when it becomes a habitual role. Sacrificial acts have meaning only in specific, limited situations, when they are performed by persons living in harmony with themselves. Too often the example of a Christ who was "obedient unto death" (Phil 2:8) is held up for imitation, and the powerless are called to imitate his perfect obedience. If we consider the death of Jesus from the point of view of obedience alone, we might overlook the fact that a readiness to live sacrificially is possible only when a person has reached the fullest level of personal freedom: "All self-sacrifice, all self-denial, and all suffering which is expressed without this harmony, that is, simply because it has been demanded by others, is senseless and produces nothing."[11] In the proclamation of Jesus, obedience is not viewed according to an authoritarian model. The goal of maintaining the established order was never his; he set about changing the world. What Jesus wanted for all persons was wholeness and well-being (see Lk 4:18–20; Gal 3:28).

Suffering and God's Will

Many women and children who take their faith seriously come to believe that their suffering is willed by God. In *The Cry of Tamar,* an excellent discussion of violence against women, Pamela Cooper-White summarizes well the essential message of hope that should be said clearly and directly to any victim of violent trauma:

1. *I believe you.*

2. *This should never have happened to you. It is not God's will for you.*

137

3. *This is not your fault.*

4. *You have choices now. You have a right to determine what happens to you and what you want to do now.*

5. *This is what I can provide you now, and here are some other resources.*

6. *God cares about what happens to you and is with you. God's love is real.*[12]

Messages like these offer safety and support, while affirming our personal power and ability to make choices. They do not minimize the trauma, blame us, or expect us to deal with it overnight. They also acknowledge that escaping from an abusive relationship can be a long and difficult road.

Most importantly for our present reflection, these statements make clear that a victim's suffering is not deserved. Religion contributes to the problem of violence against women whenever it glorifies suffering or exhorts the victimized to bear their cross. The lament of Tashi, one of the main characters in Alice Walker's novel *Possessing the Secret of Joy*, reflects the experience of women who have known the degradation of the cross in their own bodies:

> I am a great lover of Jesus, and always have been. Still, I began to see how the constant focus on the suffering of Jesus alone excludes the suffering of others from one's view. And in my sixth year as a member of Adam's congregation, I knew I wanted my own suffering, the suffering of women and little girls, still cringing before the overpowering might and weapons of the torturers, to be the subject of a sermon. Was woman herself not the tree of life? And was she not crucified? Not in some age no one even remembers, but right now, daily, in many lands on earth.[13]

Unless violence is named for what it is, there is no space to challenge the suffering that results from injustice, to feel anger, or to take action that will change our circumstances. The cycle of violence remains uninterrupted.

In working with women who have experienced violence or abuse, I find the following beliefs about suffering crucial:

1. *God is not sending us suffering as a punishment for sins we have committed.* Nothing justifies the suffering of sexual or domestic violence. Rather, we find God in our anger and protest against injustice, in our compassion for ourselves and our movement toward hope and healing. God is present with us, suffers with us, and weeps with our pain. It is also the divine presence that empowers us to resist.

2. *Jesus moved against suffering wherever he saw it.* He named it as the power of evil in the world, not something good or desirable. Following his example, we are called to relieve suffering whenever we can. Only when we have done all we can do to end it are we to find ways to live with and find meaning in it.

3. *Jesus' death on the cross does not condone suffering or tell us it is the higher spiritual path.* Jesus' commitment was to establishing love and justice in the world. He accepted the death that came upon him rather than relinquish his call to bring these about. He was not a powerless victim sacrificed to God's will, but one who freely chose the path he walked. The cross is the Christian tree of life, symbol of Jesus' intention to bring us life in abundance.

4. *The cross is not the last word in the Christian gospel; the resurrection is.* Its message is that even in the midst of death and hopelessness, new life is possible. This is what we most need to hear when we witness the horror of violence done to us or another. Transformation, not endurance or passivity, is our stance toward violence. Marie Fortune, who has worked in this area for years, sums it up well:

> We celebrate small victories, we chip away at oppressive attitudes cast in concrete, we say no in unexpected places, we speak boldly of things deemed secret and unmentionable, we stand with those who are trapped in victimization to support their journeys to safety and healing, and we break the cycle of violence we may have known in our own lives. By refusing to endure evil and by seeking to transform suffering, we are about God's work of making justice and healing brokenness.[14]

God's longing is that no one should have to suffer such violence ever again.

Forgiveness

I treat forgiveness in the next chapter, but it is so important to the topic of abuse and violence that a few points need to be made here.

First, the turn to forgiveness typically occurs far too early in the healing process. The urge to forgive may come from persons in a woman's circle of support, especially those uncomfortable with her rage and desire for revenge. Or it may arise from a woman's own spiritual convictions about the importance of forgiveness, her discomfort with her own anger, or her belief that forgiving will bring an end to the emotional pain. But forgiveness is not the goal of healing work. If it comes, it will be at the end of what is usually a long and difficult process. Further, healing comes about as grace and the power of the Spirit. It is this Spirit that at some point enables us to let go and move on.[15]

Second, we frequently think of forgiveness as an exchange between equals. But abuse and violence always involve unequal power. Those who have studied the New Testament teaching on forgiveness note how many of the references to forgiveness have to do with those in power forgiving those within their power. The majority of New Testament references are to the forgiveness God or Jesus offers to those who have sinned; clearly they are the ones in a position of power with regard to sin. In the Our Father, forgiveness also flows from the more powerful to those over whom they have power; we are taught to pray that God will forgive our debts as we forgive those who are indebted to us (Mt 5:12; Lk 11:4).

Even Jesus, the one time he is in the weaker position, does not forgive those who are more powerful and have harmed him. Instead, from the cross he asks God, the more powerful, to forgive them.

Jesus said, "Father, forgive them; they do not know what they are doing." (Lk 23:34)

While forgiveness in the New Testament is not expected or required when the offender is higher in the power hierarchy, it is expected when the person who offends us is an equal. If a tenant has a grievance against a landlord, the tenant is not only not called upon to forgive, but in fact cannot forgive the landlord so long as that relationship exists. This means that a wife can forgive a marital wrong only as a marital equal. If a man beats his wife, the battered woman not only is not required to, but should not, forgive him as long as he thinks he had the right to do what he did.[16]

There are many reasons why women do not undertake a process of healing childhood sexual abuse until they are in midlife or later. But one aspect that strikes me is that they are now adults, more equal to the adults who perpetrated the abuse, and thus able to confront these situations as the abusers' equals. The stark difference in power that exists in childhood is no longer present. This power differential shifts even more dramatically when a parent is old and frail, and the abused person has reached emotional healing. Or after the death of a parent. Many survivors of abuse have told me that in these circumstances it is as though they are relating to a different person.

Third, forgiveness is not meant to bypass acknowledgment of the evil that has been done, the need to establish safety, and the work for justice. These, not admonitions to forgiveness, are the areas where a woman most needs the support of a larger community.

Finally, it is especially important in situations of abuse and violence to be clear that forgiveness does not mean trusting or returning to the offender. It is not the same as total reconciliation, which may not be possible.

When these different dimensions of the healing process are honored, a woman is often graced with the gift of forgiveness. It comes as her anger is worked through, as elements of justice are achieved, as she experiences the love and support of a community. The experience has been integrated and no longer has the same power in a woman's life. Forgiveness comes as release and reconnection.

How do we look squarely at so much violence and still hope? I have heard many who work with it at its worst say that what sustains them is seeing not only the darkest side of the human story, but the brightest side as well. I agree. In listening day after day to people who trust enough to share their stories with me, I have heard more than I ever wanted to know about the horrors we are capable of inflicting upon one another. I have also been privileged to see dimensions of human goodness, beauty, and courage that convince me beyond doubt that the Spirit of God is at work among us. Despite all the tragedy, there are redemption and grace.

Often in the midst of a spiritual direction session with a woman who has experienced violence, we have prayed together the lament for the daughter of Jephthah with which Phyllis Trible concludes *Texts of Terror*. Part of it reads:

> Thy daughter, O Israel, is slain upon thy high places!
>   How are the powerless fallen!
> Tell it in Ammon,
>   publish it in the streets of Rabbah;
> for the daughters of the Ammonites will not rejoice;
>   the daughters of the enemies will not exult....
>
> The daughter of Jephthah lies slain upon the high places.
> I weep for you, my little sister.
> Very poignant is your story to me;
>   your courage to me is wonderful,
>   surpassing the courage of men....[17]

Sometimes, after hearing this lament, a woman begins to compose her own laments.

Spiritual convictions are transformed in a ritual's symbolic language, which reaches both body and spirit. Many of the spiritual themes we have explored regarding women and violence are expressed in the following rite for healing from rape, found in Rosemary Ruether's *Women-Church*: a full naming of the evil of violence, faith in healing as transformation, affirmation of the body, belief in the Divine as present in healing, the support of the community in feeling anger and hope.[18]

Women assemble in a circle, with the woman who has been raped inside the circle and others facing her. Someone says:

We are here because our sister (name) has been violated. Her body, her feelings, and her spirit have all been gravely injured. We are here to mourn with her and also to cry out in anger with her. We are outraged—outraged at the hostility to women and the distortion of sexuality into violence that are all around us in patriarchal society, taking the most extreme form in rape. We are filled with grief because we don't know when the violence will end and how we can repair the damage that has been done. But we refuse to give up. We will not be defeated. We will not be intimidated and turned into fearful people unable to claim our freedom to go where we please and do what we wish.

A second person says:

We love and affirm our sister (name) who has been hurt. Although she has been injured, she is not destroyed. Although she has been demeaned, yet she has not lost her integrity. Although she has been subjected to ugliness, yet she is still beautiful. Although evil has gripped her, yet she is still good. Although lies may seek to impugn her, yet she is still truthful. We affirm her wholeness, her goodness, her truthfulness, her integrity, her beauty. We dispel the forces of destruction, of ugliness, of violence, and of lies, which seek to make her their victim.

The woman may now choose to say something about her experience, or she may prefer to remain silent or express herself in nonverbal ways.

The group now leads the woman to a ritual bath. The bath is filled with herbs and sweet-smelling flower petals. Her body is immersed and massaged with sprays of warm water. She is dried and anointed with fragrant oils and clothed in a festive dress with a crown of sage leaves and a bouquet of flowers and herbs. Reassembling in a circle around the woman, one woman facing her says:

- *(With hands on abdomen)* From violence to your body, be healed. *(Others repeat)* Be healed.
- *(With hands on breasts)* From violence to your feelings, be healed....Be healed.
- *(With hands on forehead)* From violence to your mind and spirit, be healed....Be healed.
- *(All together)* The Mother-Spirit of Original Blessing surrounds you, upholds you on all sides, flows round about you, caresses you, loves you, and wills you to be whole. Be whole, sister, be whole.

17. Forgiveness

I saw forgiveness as a healing impetus, a soothing balm, a strategy that I could personalize and apply one day at a time, one antagonist at a time, one stinging hurt at a time.

—Patricia Raybon
My First White Friend[1]

orgiveness is a hard topic for women. True, it is difficult for anyone, a strange idea in a world where vengeance and violence are increasingly the response to the slightest offense. But it presents two particular dilemmas for us as women: First, we have repeatedly been told to accept and forgive when we should have been taught to resent and resist. Further, most accounts of forgiveness presuppose a level of safety and equality that simply is not a part of our lives. We are consequently suspicious of exhortations to forgive.

Yet forgiveness is a touchstone of the religious traditions that have shaped us, whether Jewish, Christian, Buddhist, or other. And even without the impulse of their teachings we know that forgiveness is necessary if human relationships are to go on. Anger toward those who have wronged us can consume us like a fire within. Tillie Olsen uses a different metaphor for its power in the opening lines of her novella, *Tell Me a Riddle*.

> For forty-seven years they had been married. How deep back the stubborn, gnarled roots of the quarrel reached, no one could say— but only now, when tending to the needs of others no longer shackled them together, the roots swelled up visible, split the earth between them, and the tearing shook even to the children, long since grown.[2]

We know the price of lives ruled by hatred and bitterness. We see all around us, in our own lives and cities, and in Ireland, the

145

Middle East, and Bosnia, the violence that breeds yet more violence in an unending cycle of bloodshed. Harboring a hatred in our hearts conforms us to the configuration of that which we hate. We respond in kind and live according to the terms of the offender. Individuals, families, or communities locked in endless conflict become mirror images of each other.

How do we avoid being prisoners to emotions destructive of self and others, while not extinguishing those that are healthy? Or, as a woman fresh from several painful betrayals puts it:

> I've had some major learnings about the power of my own rage in these last years and I'm fascinated by how we can either harness this energy for life or be killed or kill with it. "I set before you life and death—choose life" often means to choose to name and own and work with our anger. All of this of course is contrary to our training. To know and follow Jesus is to know when to turn the other cheek and when to turn the tables in the temple.

Forgiveness is a healing process that differs greatly depending on variables such as the closeness of the relationship, the magnitude of the hurt, and the remorse of the offender. But it is helpful to understand some common aspects of the process. The following three elements are central.

Acknowledging Fully the Hurt or Injustice

We begin with the truth about what happened to us. Or as close as we can come to that truth. This step distinguishes forgiveness from excusing, condoning, or silencing the self. Forgiveness is not a rush to say something did not really occur or does not really matter. Something wrong, perhaps even seriously evil, happened to us. That acknowledgment is crucial to healing. Without it, undercurrents of pain will keep on flowing. In fact, the person who feels strong anger may be closer to forgiveness than someone who denies the existence of any wrong. We immediately recognize the difference between those who fully respond to a hurt and then get on with life, and others who seem graciously to forgive only to harbor the anger and let it fester. The facade of niceness covers a deep refusal to let go.

This is especially true with wounds we sustain in intimate relationships. Nancy Mairs conveys this powerfully in *Ordinary Time.* She is telling about her husband's disclosure that he had a two-year affair with another woman.

> "But can you forgive him?" asks our friend Father Ricardo when we seek his counsel, and I reply, without hesitation, "I already have."
> I *have?* How can this be? I have never felt more hurt than I do now. I am angry. I am bitter. I try to weep but my eyes feel blasted, although occasionally I shudder and gasp in some stone's version of crying its heart out.

The unconditional love and forgiveness she feels for her husband, George, is, she says, a gift of grace. And it is an intimation of that love and forgiveness of God that fortifies her, a grace she could not previously imagine: "Believing myself forgiven by God, I must believe George equally forgiven. And if forgiven by God, surely no less by me."[3] But this conviction coexists with recognition of her anger and pain, a full coming to terms with the wound she has sustained.

The step of acknowledgment is important because it prevents forgiveness from being simply a relinquishing of the self. In the desire to keep a relationship intact, we can retreat from and lose our own perspective. We need to be suspicious of any account of forgiveness that urges such a losing of ourselves, for then love is impossible. In the course of exploring what happened, we may come to see a different picture of events, but that is different from denying our experience at the outset and putting ourselves at risk now or in the future.

The importance of fully naming injustice is evident in a spirituality emerging out of the accumulated anger, what Korean women call the *Han,* of the exploited and powerless women of Asia. Women who have never had public space for the expression of their pent-up resentment develop a deep resignation to their lot. That is why a ritual for releasing it, the *Han-pu-ri,* is so important. The *Han-pu-ri,* led by a Shaman, is one of the few spaces where poor Korean women enact a spiritual role not dominated by male religious authorities. Women gather to release accumulated anger through a ritual dance. The *Han-pu-ri* embraces three important steps: (1) *Speaking and hearing.* The Shaman gives the *Han*-ridden persons or spirits the chance to break their silence, to let their *Han* out publicly. The Shaman asks the community to hear the *Han*-ridden stories. (2) *Naming.* The Shaman next enables the *Han*-ridden persons to name the source of their oppression. (3) Changing the unjust situation so that the *Han*-ridden persons or spirits can have peace.[4]

Hurtful events encode themselves as memories in our bodies and minds. If we try simply to forgive and forget, we leave ourselves vulnerable to a similar hurt in the future. Knowing that memories will persist for a long time, our aim is to both acknowledge them and work to bring about something new. While we forgive, we may also say: "Never again will I knowingly allow this to happen." For major betrayals and crimes against us, we may need to attend to the naming and processing of the event for a very long time. But, even after such major offenses, at some point we sense ourselves opening to something new.

Cynthia Crowner, director of Kirkridge, shares a moving image of this in a reflection appearing in the retreat center's newsletter, *The Ridgeleaf.* While walking in the woods one morning, she says she noticed something she had not seen before:

> A white granite boulder had some time ago tumbled down the mountain, lodging itself into the side of a sapling. The wound of the impact was still very visible. Over time, the tree had accommodated itself to the intrusive presence of that rock by growing around it so that the rock was now embraced by the tree. In spite of that wound, the tree has continued to grow straight and tall, its higher branches forming part of the overall forest canopy as it reaches toward the light.[5]

Crowner muses on the way this wounded/healing tree speaks to her of all those she has met at Kirkridge who have transcended their wounds, healing them over a very long period of time. Grace is present at every step of this process.

The first spiritual checkpoint in the process of healing is often the desire for revenge. We imagine ourselves paying the person back or hurting them in return: "I'll teach Sally a lesson." "I want to prove that I am right." As Jungian analyst Helen Luke says in *Woman, Earth and Spirit*, every time we are hurt or angry, whether it be with a person, a circumstance, or a material thing, there is born a desire to inflict an equivalent hurt, even when we are not conscious of it: "We have suffered a little death and the desire to kill follows, for it is the nature of the psyche to seek always a restored balance."[6] But the past cannot be remade through vengeance and violence.

In *The Human Condition,* the Jewish philosopher Hannah Arendt ponders why this is so.[7] Arendt, who fled Nazi Germany in her thirties and then worked in France to relocate dispossessed Jewish refugee children, was no stranger to evil writ large. However, she believes forgiveness applies primarily not to evil on a large scale, but to the trespassing that is an everyday occurrence. Perhaps she was thinking especially of friendship, for someone remarked at her funeral that she had "a genius for friendship." She considered her friendships the center of her life, and her relating was marked by loyalty and generosity. But she was also known to be impatient and exacting in her judgments.

Arendt sees forgiveness, both that which we extend and that which we receive, as making it possible for us to go on living day after day, redeemed from what she calls the predicament of irreversibility. This is the fact that we cannot undo what we have done even though we may not have fully realized what we were doing at the time. Without being forgiven and thereby released from the consequences of what we have done, our capacity to act would be reduced to one single deed from which we could never recover. We would have to bear its consequences forever. It is forgiveness that makes it possible for life to go on by constantly releasing us from the past. Only through this constant mutual release can we find the freedom to live into the future openly.

It is for this reason that Arendt sees forgiveness as the exact opposite of vengeance. Vengeance perpetuates the original trespass in such a way that everyone remains bound to the process. Far from putting an end to the consequences of the first misdeed, which is what we hope it will do, revenge allows the chain reaction found in every action to follow its course unhindered. Only forgiveness enables us to act freely. This is because revenge is the natural and expected reaction to a wrong. Forgiveness, on the other hand, can never be predicted. It does not re-act, but acts in a new and unexpected way. Since it is not conditioned by the action that provoked it, the forgiveness contained in Jesus' teaching frees both the one who forgives and the one who is forgiven from its consequences. Vengeance, Arendt believes, locks both into a relentless process that never comes to an end.

The release Arendt talks about is vividly described in Patricia Raybon's *My First White Friend*. Raybon, a black journalist and college professor, describes the hatred of white people that simmered beneath her smiling facade. It was "an itch I'd...picked at so long I was bloody in my soul from the worry and rattle of it."[8] In a bimonthly column she wrote for the *Rocky Mountain News,* she spewed out that hate, dressing it up sometimes in a "pretty" way. And the response was just as hateful. But, she says, no lives got changed and no institutions were reformed through the hate. Later the column got canceled, and she began writing for other publications, but with a different voice. The response she got reflected the difference. Letters arrived from all over in which readers told her that her writing was prompting them to look at all their relationships.

Raybon comes to the conclusion that she can no longer bear hating people with whom she shares a nation. While it was hurting white people, she says, it was killing her. Realizing this, she got on her knees and prayed, telling God that she could not see a way out. One of the convictions that came to her was this: "Forgiveness just isn't a one-time thing. It's a God thing. And God, as I understand Her, has a long arm and a heart for mercy. God, as I see Him, isn't so stingy as to hold back a second chance. God, indeed, doesn't want to lose us to confusion."[9] Raybon came to understand forgiveness as a decision about how to live her life. Though she still gets angry, she believes that through a willingness to forgive the faults of others, she began to make peace with her own.

Though most of us will not face the magnitude of hurt Raybon knew as a black growing up in a racist society, we encounter other wounding that evokes the urge to get even. Three approaches help loosen the grip of this desire for revenge. All work best in the context of prayer, since we may encounter deep resistance to them even in smaller matters.

The first is recognition of our own need for forgiveness. A woman who struggles with the fear and anger she feels about the way she is treated as a lesbian reflects after an election in which an antidiscrimination initiative had been roundly defeated: "What will it do to me if I don't move beyond it? People like the Dalai Lama and Thich Nhat Hanh suggest to me another way. I know how to be angry, frustrated, and vindictive. Can I also reach for something that includes that hurt but is larger? I know I am also a bigot in many ways." Part of forgiveness is the realization of our own capacity to wound, as well as the embrace of our common humanity.[10]

A second approach is seeing the experience from the perspective of the person whose behavior we are trying to forgive. This means standing in the person's shoes for a time. We can do this by asking ourselves several questions[11]:

What need might influence the person to act this way?

What beliefs or values are at work in the person?

What aspects of the person's history (hurts, losses, cultural and religious formation) are part of this behavior?

What limitations (fears, present problems, lack of skills) play a part?

Imagine a dialogue between yourself and the other person. You state your position and then imagine the other person answering. Go back and forth between your attack and the other person's defense at least three times. Notice how your feelings begin to change as you hear the other person's unique experience.

A third approach is deciding simply to let the offense go, being clear about what this means. Reflection on several questions helps with this decision.[12]

Is this worth being upset about?

Is this really what's upsetting me, or am I upset about other things and blowing it out of proportion?

How important is this in the big picture?

What is my level of commitment to this person or relationship?

What do I stand to gain by holding on to my anger? By letting it go?

There are different ways of letting go. One is internal: We cease rehearsing and going over the wrongdoing. Refraining as much as possible from inner rehearsals of the hurt enables it to recede in importance. Rituals of release help. Recently a friend called to say she had landed a good job she had been working toward for some weeks. She was leaving a position where she had been treated unfairly the previous two years. They were difficult years, but she had needed the job and could not simply quit. Now she wanted to move on: "I want to go to a healing service at my church. They have one every two weeks. I don't want to carry all this with me. I think it will harm my body and mind."

Although we work at it, this kind of release often comes as a gift. One woman describes how this happened for her:

> It was about the time I was letting go of all my anger toward my sister-in-law. I had never had such hatred and I had carried it a long time. She hadn't been very nice to me, but I didn't like the feeling— it felt awful. It was just *lifted* from me. It was such a release. She was here visiting and I had decided to take her to the doctor. She said some nice things about me to the doctor. At the same time I was letting go, she was changing.

Another kind of letting go is to accept that the situation is not going to change and we will have to find ways to live with it. Railing against it only produces unhappiness. The overall picture warrants this kind of acceptance.

Letting go may mean ending a relationship, facing the fact that a situation or relationship is unrewarding or toxic. It will not change and is costing more than I can emotionally sustain. In such cases I must be willing to pay the price of letting go: loss, money fears, guilt, loneliness, disapproval, or rejection.

Because, as women, we take primary responsibility for relationships and value connection so highly, we may assume that if we were better there would not be a problem. We tend to keep trying harder. Letting go may free us to mourn the loss of a relationship and move on.

Balancing the Demands of Forgiveness and Justice

Forgiveness is linked to justice and repentance. If there is to be a new relationship, it needs to be free of the former evil. In fact, the fullness of forgiveness may not be possible until justice happens. The person who has hurt us cannot simply say, "I'm sorry you feel that way." They must accept responsibility: "What I did was wrong, and I am sorry." But words are not enough to restore the trust that has been broken. The person must refrain from further injustice.

That is why forgiveness does not necessarily lead to full reconciliation, since that calls for the participation of both parties. Do we reestablish contact? Set new boundaries? Reconciliation implies a fresh start. There are therefore situations when reconciliation is simply not possible because the offender is unrepentant, vicious, or dangerous.

Women throughout the world are searching for fresh ways to balance the demands of forgiveness and justice. A few years ago Dr. Elizabeth Menkin spoke at the Seattle Mennonite Church. In that lecture she told how, after a drunken driver killed her sister, she wanted something that the legal system could not offer: a chance to talk directly with the driver. The woman had pleaded guilty to killing Elizabeth's sister Elaine in a head-on collision. When the accident occurred, her blood-alcohol level was twice the legal limit for drunkenness. Menkin and her family arranged to meet with her in a motel room, working with a professional mediator from Mediation Services for Victims and Offenders, a nonprofit organization based in Seattle. The first visit lasted four and a half hours and was followed by letters and more visits in jail.

It led the woman to take responsibility for the death and pledge to do what she could to avoid becoming a repeat offender. For Menkin's family it brought a sense of relief from the anger they had not been able to get rid of before. "I felt this enormous release that I didn't have to kill her," Menkin said about meeting the woman. "It was important for me to have eye-to-eye contact. To see her tears, her hands tremble. I have come to understand how I can be at peace in spite of the crime."[13]

Other efforts are being made today to find a justice that somehow leads to healing. The Truth and Reconciliation Commission in South Africa is perhaps the most prominent of these, since it works at a national level. Due to Nelson Mandela's leadership, South Africa continues a way of reconciliation that is courageous and amazing, given the vicious system of racial oppression that previously existed. In 1996, Mandela's administration established the Commission to provide a public forum for the private grief of the millions of perpetrators and victims of violence in South Africa. Its goal is to encourage truth telling about what happened during the years of apartheid so that, through hearing that truth, people can mourn and heal.

The key concept behind the Commission is *ubuntu,* a word familiar to South Africans but difficult to translate. *Ubuntu* is the belief that we do not exist without our neighbors and, since people are defined by their relationships with others, healing is the responsibility of everyone. In the traditions of African tribal society, *ubuntu* means that no one is ever fully human except in community with others. The Commission is therefore founded on faith in community.

There are moving moments in the hearings. A community leader recalls:

> One of our neighbors had been suffering and unable to work. We told her she needed to come to church and tell her story. Reluctantly, she came. But as she stood in front of us, she was overcome by shaking so bad that she was unable to speak. So the congregation sang to her. The melody of our song and the strength of

our voices filled the church. Eventually, she was able to resume speaking. She told of the horror of seeing her teenage son's body and realizing he was dead. Her body started shaking again so badly that she could not continue. We sang to her again. That day she told her story for the first time, surrounded by the voices of her community. Her heart was still broken, yet her spirit began to heal.[14]

Not all choose to deal with the violence by returning to memories. Many homes were destroyed in the community of Mambi when it was attacked repeatedly by government forces. When workers from the Survivors of Violence team asked the local women who had lost their homes what the organization could do for them, the women replied that they wanted a garden. The trauma workers, who did not know the least thing about gardening, were taken aback by the modesty and seeming irrelevance of the request. But the women knew. They formed a support group around the gardening. While they gardened, they sang together. They talked about their losses as they weeded and harvested the area. The fruit and vegetables grew, were harvested, and taken to market. They were able to generate an income, which was very empowering.[15]

While no one knows whether irreparable damage from the dark days of oppression and injustice will ultimately drag the process in South Africa to a halt, many are committed to it. Meanwhile, it challenges the hearts and imaginations of all those throughout the world seeking a way to justice beyond either passivity or violence.

Forgiveness is a restorative event, and such restoration is finally the work of the Spirit. As such it is supported by communities of faith and liturgies that prepare us to receive that Spirit. One of the ways such newness also opens out to us is through the inspiration of those who make the healing journey sooner and further than we are presently able. Their stories witness to a larger possibility, even as we struggle with our own issues in living out the meaning of forgiveness. Such witnessing occurred at a conference on violence against women held in San Juan, Costa Rica. The conference participants heard the story of Noh Soo-Bock, a Korean comfort woman for Japanese soldiers during the Second World War. In her old age, Noh Soo-Bock was able to say, "Korean, Japanese,

Chinese, Thai are not different. We are all friends!" The theologian who was presenting Noh Soo-Bock's story pondered: Where did she find this power for forgiveness? What made her choose to forgive the Japanese? Was it the teachings on compassion and loving-kindness found in her Buddhist faith? Or the experience of being loved by Malaysian, Chinese, and Thai in her new homeland? The presenter cannot answer these questions but is moved by the witness of such a life. She sees that Noh Soo-Bock has broken the vicious cycle of violence and revenge with her power. Her legacy is one of survival, forgiveness, and acceptance: "Her forgiveness was her best revenge, and her acceptance was her best resistance."[16] Like others who struggle with the many paradoxes at the heart of forgiveness, Noh Soo-Bock shows us that it can be a life-sustaining, liberating, and transforming grace.

18. *Loving Enemies*

"Love of enemies" cannot mean a forgiveness that ignores injustices or loses the perspective that there are enemies. This is probably the most important task for women.

—Karen Labacqz
"Love Your Enemy"[1]

n our home office shelf is a calligraphy piece from our wedding announcement. It is the familiar passage on love from 1 Corinthians 13:7:

> Love forgives all things,
> believes all things,
> hopes all things,
> endures all things.

The scripture passage goes on to talk about how love is patient and kind, and knows no evil. I did not think too much about the full implications of the quotation when we first selected it as a wedding text. Now, after years of sitting with women in that office and listening to their stories, the passage has begun to trouble me more and more. I have a new awareness of what it means when women attempt to make these and other New Testament texts the touchstone of their lives: Love your enemies. Do good to those who hate you. Pray for those who persecute you. Do not repay evil with evil. Turn the other cheek (Mt 5).

The "enemy" appears in diverse guises: the colleague who undermines my reputation at work, the family member who criticizes everything I do, the drunken driver responsible for my daughter's death, the white people who get the lion's share of economic and housing resources. A young college student tells how her uncle harasses her at family gatherings until she is at the point of tears: "I try to be especially nice to him because I hate him so much." Women ask me: How am I supposed to love the husband who left me for another woman? the father who repeatedly abused me? "What is the meaning of love," one asks, "when I deserve to be angry or even to hate someone for what they have done to me?"

We live in a world of connections marked not only by goodness and grace, but by evil and sin. For women, the issue of loving enemies raises the question: How do we live the gospel and at the same time assure our own safety and survival?

Jesus' Message: The Search for a Middle Way

Jesus' teachings have often seemed like impractical idealism. "Turn the other cheek" implies a doormatlike passivity, which is precisely what women need to reject. "Do not repay evil with evil" seems to counsel cowardice and submission.

Yet Jesus never behaved in these ways. Nor did he tell his oppressed listeners not to resist evil. His entire ministry speaks to the contrary. If we view the New Testament teachings about enemies not as isolated statements but in light of Jesus' whole life, their meaning is more like: "Do not strike back at evil with evil. Do not give blow for blow. Do not retaliate against violence with violence."[2] The key element lies in the means to be used: How are we to resist evil? Neither by passivity, nor by returning violence for violence. We are to find another way.

To understand what this means, it is helpful to read the Matthew passage about enemies in context.

> You have heard that it was said, "An eye for an eye and a tooth for a tooth." But I say to you, Do not resist an evildoer. But if anyone strikes you on the right cheek, turn the other also; and if anyone wants to sue you and take your coat, give your cloak as well; and if anyone forces you to go one mile, go also the second mile. (5:38–41, NRSV)

First, note that a blow that is to land on the right cheek requires using the left hand. Now in Jesus' society, the left hand was used only for unclean tasks. To strike the right cheek with the right hand would mean using the back of the hand. This is unmistakably an insult. The intention is not to injure, but to humiliate, to put someone in his or her place. This was the normal way of admonishing inferiors. One did not normally strike a peer at all, and doing so brought an exorbitant fine. But masters did in fact backhand slaves, as husbands did wives, parents did children, and men did women.

It is important to remember that Jesus' audience consisted of those who were subjected to constant indignities, those forced to stifle their outrage at the dehumanizing treatment they received, a humiliated people. So why turn the other cheek? Because it is a way of saying: I deny you the power to humiliate me. You cannot demean me. What is the striker to do? To hit with a fist makes the person an equal. The striker, stripped of the power to dehumanize the other, has been forced to regard the person as an equal human being. Now he or she has a different choice. Jesus' teaching offers a way of opposing evil without mirroring it. What Jesus is asking us to do is to find creative alternatives between fight or flight, violence or submission.[3]

The solution we find should not be a refusal of strength. It should bring into play another kind of power. Anger and hatred are not denied, but confronted and eventually overcome and transcended. As we have seen, righteous anger not only helps us maintain our self-worth, it enables us to resist violence and abuse from others. There can be no love of enemies that bypasses honest moral and political judgment.

Protecting Ourselves: The Power of Intuition

Loving our enemies does not mean putting ourselves in dangerous situations or trusting those who are not worthy of our trust. Jesus called the Pharisees snakes and drove the merchants out of the temple. He sometimes avoided Jerusalem, knowing his life was in danger there. Love is not the same as failing to recognize that there are enemies. We need to exercise discernment in determining whether to treat others with kindness or caution.

Not long ago several Seattle women gave generously to a clean-cut young man who walked the city streets with a map and posed as a distraught traveler. Apparently anxious and confused, he stopped them to ask for directions. Then he told his story. He was a British student heading back to London after traveling around the West Coast. He misread the flight time on his ticket and missed his plane. He needed to pay about fifty dollars to change his ticket to get that night's flight. But he had spent all his money and was searching for an emergency services office where the airline told him he could get some help.

The women tried to figure out how to help this stranded youth. Some bought him lunch. Some offered to lend him money so he could get a flight home. He vowed to pay them back as soon as he got home, and gave them his name, address, and phone number in England, as well as his mother's name and his passport number. But later they discovered that he was not a stranded traveler at all. He was a con artist who had been hanging around Seattle for months. At least three dozen women are known to have given him money.

Seattle Times travel reporter Kristin Jackson was one of those women: "As I talked to him, I did have a few doubts. (When I asked to see his airline ticket and passport he said he'd left them in an airport locker with his luggage—which no real traveler would do). But he was young, just about twenty-two, and inexperienced, I told myself. And confused and upset like anyone stranded in a foreign country would be. He needed help. So I ignored my doubts and loaned him fifty dollars, reasoning either I'd end up with a heart-warming story of a traveler who was helped by strangers—and repaid the loan. Or I'd end up with the story of a travel scam. I ended up with this tale of a scam—a story of a grinch of a man."[4]

In *The Gift of Fear,* his discussion of the signals that protect us from violence, Gavin de Becker makes clear how important intuition is. He believes it is a powerful internal resource for survival; it has saved a number of his clients' lives. De Becker's firm advises many of the world's most prominent government and media figures, corporations, and law enforcement agencies on predicting violence. It deals as well with ordinary citizens who are victims of domestic abuse and stalking. Intuition, knowing something without knowing exactly how, is a gift we all have. But often we ignore it, hiding its information from ourselves. What gets in the way of using our intuition, de Becker believes, is negative judgment. We disregard intuition unless we can explain it logically, and we judge our feelings rather than honoring them.

When it comes to protecting ourselves from violence, one judgment we need to ignore is that we are being rude. Faced with a man who could not take no for an answer, a woman said: "It just didn't seem very charitable if I didn't at least keep listening to him." De Becker encourages women to explicitly rebuff unwanted approaches. He insists that women must learn how to explicitly reject and say no, and to take that power early in a relationship. De Becker knows this is difficult to do in a culture where women are expected to be warm and open.

> It is understandable that the perspectives of men and women on safety are so different—men and women live in different worlds. I don't remember where I first heard this simple description of one dramatic contrast between the genders, but it is strikingly accurate: At core, men are afraid women will laugh at them, while at core, women are afraid men will kill them."[5]

And we need to learn not to override our fear because a person seems nice. As de Becker says, "'He was so nice' is a comment I often hear from people describing the man who, moments or months after his niceness, attacked them. We must learn and then teach our children that niceness does not equal goodness. Niceness is a decision, a strategy of social interaction; it is not a character trait."[6]

Intuition has long been seen as a feminine quality, and for that reason, usually dismissed. Now research is showing that it is crucial in making good decisions. Decision making requires two parallel but interacting mental activities. One involves activating a brain circuit that stores knowledge about a person's emotional experiences, his or her intuition. That part of the brain sends signals to other parts of the brain, which recall the overall facts of a situation, including various options. These use the unconscious knowledge, the intuition, to make the right decision.[7]

How does the truth of intuition come to us? Some of its signals are: nagging feelings, persistent thoughts, humor, anxiety, hunches, gut feelings, doubt, hesitation, suspicion, apprehension, fear. In *Dwellings: A Spiritual History of the Living World*, Linda Hogan says that intuition is an inner knowing, one of the laws we carry deep within us: "It's a blood-written code that directs us through life."[8] It is rooted in a recognition of our sensuality and its power. We feel the environment and we send out clues that others sense. We, in turn, understand through the senses. If we learn to listen to this bodily wisdom, we are better equipped to know and name the enemies in our midst.

Cultivating Loving-Kindness

Once we have become discerning about the existence of evil, we are ready to turn again to the meaning of love. The Buddhist tradition contains a 2,500-year-old practice that is helpful in moving beyond certain kinds of hatred and anger; it may or may not apply to your situation. It is a meditation on loving-kindness that uses the repetition of phrases, images, and feelings to evoke friendliness toward oneself and others. It is meant to release us from our hatred, hurt feelings, and guilt, and open our hearts to ourselves and others. It is done for fifteen or twenty minutes once or twice a day.

Find a quiet place and a comfortable position. Then relax your body and mind, letting go as much as possible any tension and preoccupations. Then recite inwardly the following phrases directed to yourself. You begin with yourself, because love of others is rooted in this love of self. Buddhists teach that our love is not genuine if we do not care equally for ourselves.

May I be filled with loving-kindness.
May I be well.
May I be peaceful and at ease.
May I be happy.

Let the phrases circle through you again and again, permeating your body and mind. If it is helpful, image yourself held in a heart of loving-kindness, the womb of God, the mantle of divine care, or another image that speaks to you. Give yourself some weeks, or as long as you need, to let this loving-kindness for yourself grow.

When you feel ready, expand your meditation to include others beyond yourself. Begin with those you love. Picture them and use the following phrases to evoke a sense of loving-kindness for them.

May you be filled with loving-kindness.
May you be well.
May you be peaceful and at ease.
May you be happy.

Finally, try including the most difficult people in your life. Give yourself time for this power of loving-kindness to connect you more fully with the entire universe of living beings. Try using it in traffic jams, while waiting in line at the grocery store, or as you prepare for difficult encounters. It honors the connections among us, and has power to calm and center the heart.[9]

19. Women and Nonviolent Resistance

Nonviolence...is about speaking the whole complicated truth, responding to the fullness of the struggle, and it requires my most bitter words, my most hearty laughter, my deepest compassion, my sharpest wit.

—Pam McAllister
You Can't Kill the Spirit[1]

ometimes it is hard to acknowledge anger because we have no idea what to do with it. At such times it helps to remember the long history of women's nonviolent struggle for change. Within this legacy we find not only inspiration and practical ideas, but renewed hope that it is actually possible to make a difference.

Such plotting to outwit historical circumstances starts in the earliest books of the Bible. The Book of Exodus begins with the story of women's behind-the-scenes engineering to save Moses and an entire generation of Israelites. Determined to do the will of God, midwives Shiphrah and Puah refuse to obey the royal order to kill all Hebrew boys at birth. Moses' mother, Jochebed, hides him. When that is no longer possible, she devises a watertight boat of branches and reeds to cradle him. The Pharaoh wants all Hebrew boys thrown in the Nile. In a nice touch of irony, Moses is in the Nile, but not in the way the Pharaoh envisioned. Instead of being exposed to drowning, he floats in a little ark. Pharaoh's daughter, who comes to bathe in the Nile, spots the ark and has compassion for the crying infant inside. She also violates her father's edict and saves Moses from the river. Moses' sister, Miriam, presents a timely suggestion, "Shall I go and call you a nurse from the Hebrew women to nurse the child for you?" As a final irony, Moses' mother thus ends up being paid to nurse her own child. Women's wit, humor, compassion, and courage set in motion Israel's liberation from bondage in Egypt.

When we think of the history of nonviolence, Mohandas Gandhi and Martin Luther King, Jr., not Lucretia Mott and Fannie Lou Hamer, come immediately to mind. Women's contributions are not fully included, certainly not highlighted, in most discussions of nonviolence. However, we are becoming more aware of how extensive these have been. I choose one contemporary story that has had impact throughout the world. With it in mind, we can then reflect on the meaning and tactics of nonviolence as they relate to our use of anger.

The Mothers of the Disappeared

From the time of the military coup in 1976, children in Argentina had been disappearing. If they raised their fists, their voices, or their eyebrows, they disappeared. If they joined a union, sang freedom songs, or were seen in the wrong place at the wrong time, they disappeared. Occasionally, even if they had done nothing wrong at all, they disappeared. More than 10,000 people, probably as many as 30,000, disappeared in Argentina between 1976 and 1979. Half of them were under the age of thirty. There were no bodies nor proof of torture, no world outrage. Only heavy footsteps at night and muffled screams.

For a mother of one of these "disappeared" there was no word of what had happened to her child, no funeral or closure, no opportunity to grieve and heal. Many of these mothers went to the Ministry of the Interior in Buenos Aires daily, hungry for information. They waited in long barren corridors. When a woman finally met with an official, she was told that her child had likely run off, abandoned the family, or joined a terrorist group someplace. The officials told the mother to go home. Still, day after day, the mothers waited.

Azucena De Vicenti, a woman well into her sixties, was one of the women rudely dismissed by the officials. She was angry. And as she passed the other waiting mothers on the way out, she said: "It's not here we ought to be—it's the Plaza de Mayo. And when there's enough of us, we'll go to the Casa Rosada and see the president about our children who are missing."[2]

165

The next Saturday, April 13, 1977, fourteen women decided to stand together as witnesses to the disappearance of their children. Although public demonstrations were forbidden, they came separately to the Plaza de Mayo, wearing flat shoes in case they had to run. The square was deserted on Saturday afternoons, so the women next decided to gather on Thursdays, when the Plaza was crowded. They walked every week in a slow-moving circle around the square, carrying pictures of their lost loved ones. People started calling them "the Mothers of the Plaza," or *"las locas de la Plaza"*–"the mad women." Hebe Pastori Bonafini had two sons, both of whom were in their twenties when they disappeared: "Every morning when I wake up, I think only about my sons and about what I can do to take them from where they are. It is as if lions grew inside of me, and I am not afraid."[3]

When the women realized that the newspapers were afraid to write about their actions, they raised enough money to buy an advertisement. It appeared, in spite of efforts of the military to stop it, in *La Prensa* on October 5, 1977. Above pictures of 237 "disappeared" and the names of their mothers was the headline, WE DO NOT ASK FOR ANYTHING MORE THAN THE TRUTH.

When the women began gathering signatures for a petition and holding open meetings, severe police repression followed. Hundreds of people were harassed, arrested, and detained. A dozen of the women, including Azucena De Vicenti, were kidnapped and disappeared forever. For a time it became impossible to maintain their presence in the Plaza, but in churches around the city the mothers continued to gather. They lit candles and paused in the pews to rest and pray. Meanwhile, as their heads were bowed, they passed notes to one another, making decisions in the dark sanctuaries without speaking a word.

In 1980 the women returned to the Plaza, wearing flat shoes and white scarves embroidered with the names or initials of the relatives they were seeking. Although they faced police tear gas, nightsticks, and arrest, they were determined not to retreat again into silence and shadows. They continue to walk in the Plaza. Says Maria Adela Gard de Antonkoletz, vice president of the Mother's Organization: "At first each mother thinks that she is alone, that she is the only one. Little by little she comes to understand what has happened in our country. Then she changes and searches not only for her son, but for all our children. We work for all the children."[4] When asked if they think the perpetrators of crimes against their children will be legally tried and put in jail, they respond no. But, they say, at least we are the living memory. In addition, the Mothers of the Disappeared inspired women in other countries where children were disappearing.

The Meaning of Nonviolence

In a world that too easily divides people into categories of *them* and *us*, nonviolence respects the complex truths of most situations in which we find ourselves, truths such as these: Each of us is at times both oppressor and oppressed. The system of patriarchy is evil, but we love our fathers, sons, brothers, husbands, and male friends. People do not fit into simple categories of good and evil. Nonviolence enables us to honor such complex mixtures of good and evil in this way: It asks us to become clear both about what we refuse to accept from others and what we can respect in them or have in common with them—even though at times that may be very little.

Barbara Deming, whose life and work were dedicated to nonviolence, has a helpful image for this. She speaks of the two hands of nonviolence. She believed that we put two pressures on the oppressor, our defiance of him and our respect for him. In other words, with one hand we say to the antagonist: "Stop what you are doing. I refuse to obey or cooperate with you and your demands. I will even interfere with the wrong you are doing." With the other, we deliver the message: "You are not the other, and I am not the other. I will not cast you out of the human race."[5]

Mohandas Gandhi coined the term *satyagraha* to describe nonviolent social change. *Satya* (truth) plus *agraha* (force) equals "truth force," or the force of truth. *Force* here refers to the power of active nonviolence. Regarding *truth,* Gandhi emphasized that each of us holds some truth, but none of us holds absolute truth. The essence of conflict is the search for truth; the goal for all parties in a conflict is to come to an enlarged truth, a shared truth.[6]

If truth is the goal, nonharm, or *ahimsa*, is the way to pursue it. By harming you I both destroy something of the truth you embody and at the same time diminish the truth of my own self. Nonviolence is sometimes misunderstood as passivity and weakness. It actually requires great courage. As Gandhi emphasized: "*Ahimsa* is an attribute of the brave. Cowardice and *ahimsa* do not go together any more than water and fire."[7] But we refuse to harm or dehumanize our enemies.

True nonviolent resistance is not possible until we have learned to acknowledge and express anger in healthy ways. Nonviolence is not the same as suppressing an emotion because of fear, intimidation, or censorship. We do not choose nonviolence because we are afraid to fight. Pam McAllister, author of several fine works on women and nonviolence, tells of a time she was being interviewed on a radio talk show in New York City. A listener called at the end of the show to chide her, saying that an advocate of nonviolence should not be angry. The talk show host quickly reassured the caller that Pam was really very sweet and not at all angry. Pam thanked her for defending her, but said she considered her anger both a sign of her health and essential to her life as an advocate of nonviolence: "It is evidence of my love for life. Without the anger I'd probably be silent as stone, passive, complacent."[8]

How do I resist if another does not practice nonviolence and, instead, inflicts harm on me? This is the crucial question for women. To passively endure the suffering is not caring of self; to retaliate in kind is not nonviolence. But violence leads to ever deepening circles of violence; we see evidence of this throughout the world today. Evil has to be fought with courage and tenacity. Christian love, carried out through nonviolence, is a powerful force for doing this. At no other time have we been as ready as a society to try nonviolence. We are beginning to realize that unless we can live with simple decency toward one another, we might all be destroyed.

Tactics for Bringing about Change Nonviolently

Even without naming it as such, we often use nonviolent tactics in practice: making a phone call, writing a letter, signing a petition,

168

going on strike, taking part in a boycott, joining a demonstration or participating in a silent candlelight vigil. These basic tactics of non-violence have been divided into three categories: (1) *Nonviolent protest and persuasion.* These actions name what is wrong and try to help others understand. Such tactics include picketing, demonstrating, lobbying, and petitioning. (2) *Nonviolent noncooperation.* With these actions we refuse to participate in the wrong we have named. We boycott, go on strike, use tax resistance. (3) *Nonviolent intervention.* We step into the way of the wrong we have named; we interfere or block it through blockades, civil disobedience, and sit-ins.[9] Categories like these help us think about nonviolence, but they don't begin to exhaust all the ways it can be expressed.

In her discussion of women's environmental activism, Rose Marie Berger shows how almost all the major grassroots environmental movements in the United States were started and led by women.

> Women-led community-based movements were strong, effective, and hard to break because of one-on-one conversations, women's intimate connectedness and personal experience with the issues, and their desire to build solid relationships around the information they gained.[10]

For example, in 1888 Jane Addams founded Hull House in Chicago, which became a kind of underground university for woman activists concerned about questions of housing, sanitation, and public health. The most severe problem in the neighborhood was inadequate garbage collection. The women from Hull House began a major investigation into the city's garbage collection system. Then Addams submitted her own bid to collect garbage, and the mayor was forced to appoint her as garbage inspector for her ward. The Hull House women formed a garbage patrol, mapping routes and dump sites, and making citizens' arrests of landlords whose properties were health hazards. Their vigilance moved garbage reform to the top of Chicago's civic agenda.

One tactic not always recognized as such, but often used by women, is singing. A number of African American spirituals were veiled protest songs that announced secret meetings and plans for escape.

> Steal away, steal away,
> Steal away to Jesus!
> Steal away, steal away home,
> I ain't got long to stay here.

These spirituals also described the route and risk of the freedom trail. For Harriet Tubman, as well as other conductors on the Underground Railroad, songs were used as coded messages to alert people that she was in the area and ready to move.[11]

The African American civil rights activist Fannie Lou Hamer used her skills as a song leader to convey her own suffering and that of her people. In the 1960s she led a version of the Christmas spiritual "Go Tell It on the Mountain" during a Mississippi Freedom Democratic Party mass meeting, editing the text so that she sang,

> Go tell it on the mountain,
> Over the hills and everywhere,
> Go tell it on the mountain,
> To let my people go!

By keeping the original melody, the song reminds singers of the joy of the birth of Christ, which also calls for the rebirth of the singers. One of Hamer's most moving performances is the spiritual-derived "This Little Light of Mine":

> This little light of mine, I'm gonna let it shine,
> This little light of mine, I'm gonna let it shine,
> This little light of mine, I'm gonna let it shine,
> Let it shine, let it shine, let it shine.

It was more than a song for Fannie Lou Hamer; it was a means of sacred and political action.[12]

Women's groups continue to use songs that allow us to celebrate our lives and work for change. They are one of the ways we remain visible and serve notice that we do not plan to disappear. Our groups also incorporate, sometimes in their very names, another nonviolent tactic not always recognized as such: humor. In the wonderful collection of Jewish women's commentaries on the Book of Ruth, *Reading Ruth,* a contributor describes her group. Five women, with ages spanning the late twenties to fifties, meet in a Manhattan living room. They are members of an ongoing group facetiously acronymed WGTDTB: Women Gathered to Deplore the Bible. One or two women secretly wish the initials connoted something more innocent, like Women Gathered to Discuss the Bible. However, when a mailing went out under that rubric, too few responded.[13] Nonviolence that is to be sustained over time requires not only courage, honesty, and discipline, but humor as well.

20. Anger and Creativity

> I am a God of a thousand names:
> why cannot one of them be
> Woman Singing?
> — Catherine de Vinck
> "The Womanly Song of God"[1]

eading a friend's moving account of using art in her work with immigrant children, I would never have guessed it was anger that gave birth to the project. It is a fine example of using angry energy to create something beautiful.

With the politics at school, anger is a constant emotion I have to deal with and the angrier I get, the more creative I have to become to channel the emotion so that rather than becoming destructive, I become more life-giving. Often there is nothing I can do about colleagues who are insecure, jealous or judgmental. No manner of reaching out will do for those who close their doors and refuse to engage in dialogue. At times I feel I have to "eat" my anger or explode.

But I have found a way. Here is one example. A year or so ago, I had legitimately missed an after-school meeting when the children were assigned to classes and I ended up with thirty-one of the most difficult students to teach—an unfair assignment because all the other docile and on-grade-level students were distributed among those present at the meeting. No amount of protest would change my colleagues who stood firm by some unwritten school law, "You snooze, you lose."

I was angry for a long time and the anger was beginning to turn to rage as I realized that no one individual could meet the needs of all those children at risk. What would be the meaning or purpose of my teaching if no matter what I did, they wouldn't make it anyway? I wondered.

But then one day I had a flash of inspiration. I found a new way to work with the children. I began with art. Each day I taught them

172

how to draw, how to focus, concentrate, and develop attention to detail. While they were engaged in their artwork, I took small groups of children to the back of the room and worked with them on developing all the other skills they needed to succeed in school. As the students came alive, my anger was transformed and I put my own creative energy to work. I wrote about the experience in a chapter of a book that has just recently been published.

The book's chapter describes how well these immigrant children did academically, once they had found their muted voices in art. It also contains moving examples of their art.[2]

Anger is energy, and several wisdom traditions speak to the creative transformation of its potentially destructive force. They suggest how anger can be expressed as creativity. Aryuvedic medicine describes the difference between energy itself and the energy pattern or form, the container through which our life energy is flowing at any given time. The energy itself is the *ch'i*, or life force. Its form may be anger, joy, sorrow, or enthusiasm. In Chinese, the words for becoming angry, *sheng ch'i*, mean generating the *ch'i*, or increasing the life force. Another tradition, that of alchemy, is dedicated to turning unsatisfactory elements into useful ones. Alchemists put impure dross metals into a sealed flask, hoping to create in this darkness the conditions for their transformation into pure gold.

Contemporary science as well offers a vision of the universe in which all annihilation involves transformation into something new and vibrant. Nature's story is one of turbulence or fluctuation that brings about continual metamorphosis. Noise, disorder, and chaos are part of nature's story. We are a balancing act on the edge of chaos. All about us nature is converting random energy into new forms. As chaos theory tells us, life's systems are basically unstable. And it is their flirtation with chaos or disorder that brings about often beautiful and unpredictable novelty. Too much chaos means unbound energy that accomplishes nothing; too much rigidity brings about a stagnation that communicates nothing. Such unstable systems maintain themselves against decay and erosion by recycling energy. But they never give back energy in the same form in which it has been taken in. The more complex the system is, the more it recycles energy. It is precisely the chaos, the irregularity, that catalyzes a new level of organization. Nothing is ever lost. Rather, it continues in a changed state.[3]

Transforming anger is the process of redirecting vital passion. Too often we can see no place for it to go, and it comes beating back on us. "When a woman holds on to her rage, it becomes a poison circulating in her bloodstream," Mary Valentis and Anne Devane say in *Female Rage*. "When she transforms it, rage can become determination, creativity, courage, and passion."[4]

Using anger creatively unites us with the Spirit at work in the world to bring life out of death. The creative process itself, in both its beauty and pain, is a concrete way of experiencing the Holy. Jewish poet Marcia Falk has written a series of blessings that envisage the Divine as the force from which the world and its inhabitants draw their sustenance and creative power. Human beings are not simply passive recipients of God's graciousness, but active participants in this creative process and in the divine-human relationship itself:

> Let us bless the source of life,
> source of faith and daring,
> wellspring of new song
> and the courage to mend.
>
> It is ours to praise
> the beauty of the world
> even as we discern
> the torn world.
>
> Let us bless the source of life,
> source of darkness and light,
> heart of harmony and chaos,
> creativity and creation.[5]
>
> (THE BOOK OF BLESSINGS by Marcia Falk,
> HarperCollins Publishers, Inc.)

How do we align with these divine creative energies that mold us, that engender growth, that enliven our inner being? How do we become a bush that burns but is not consumed? There are several ways.

Using Anger to Build Creative Self-Awareness

Anger tells us what we value. In her discussion of *Women's Bodies, Women's Wisdom,* physician Christiane Northrup says she believes anger exists to let us know we are not taking the clearest path to what we want. In her medical practice, Northrup draws on both traditional medicine and alternative approaches to healing. Emotional processes are as important to her as the physical. They take us to our innermost needs, values, and priorities: Who am I? What do I value? What do I deserve? What will I do regarding this situation? For too long, we have asked instead: How can I please others? How can I win love and approval? How can I keep the peace? When we feel stuck in our anger, she recommends a six-step process to get energy flowing positively again:

1. *Recognize what I am feeling without making any judgment on it. Avoid wallowing or prolonging it, but feel it fully.*

2. *Acknowledge there is a reason I am feeling what I am.*

3. *Spend time identifying what is causing my energy to flow negatively or to be stuck.*

4. *Having identified the source of the negative emotion, ask myself what I do want. This is often difficult for women to identify, so it may take time for me to name it. But when I do, it shifts my focus back to positive thoughts and moves my energy toward what I want.*

5. *Name what I want, sometimes making a list of exactly what I want in a given situation. When I am thinking about or talking about what I want, the negative emotion often goes away by itself.*

6. *Affirm that I have the power to get what I want.*[6]

We cannot figure out what to do about a certain situation until we have gone through the entire process of looking in the direction of what we want. We remind ourselves that whenever we are reacting against something we do not want, we just create more of what is not working and our actions are based on fixing what we do not want instead of creating what we do want.

Northrup believes that this process helps us to affirm our emotions fully, and use them as inner guidance. It creates clarity before dialogue with others begins. For example: Cynthia was angry because some members of her church were forming a small group to meet over the summer. When she listened to her anger, she heard in it a fear that this group's action threatened to divide the church, and she found that discouraging. When I asked her to speak in terms of what she wanted in the situation, her voice actually became stronger: "I want what will be for the good of the whole group and not just a few. I want inclusion and not exclusiveness." The next question she began to consider was, "In light of this, what do I want to do?"

This process can be used in small or large ways. I recognize in it some of my own attempts to redirect anger. In July of 1958, the summer I graduated from Sacred Heart Academy, I joined the Sisters of the Holy Names. Twenty years later, after a long and difficult discernment process, I decided to leave the order. I made my decision believing somewhat naively that I could continue teaching theology full-time at the university level. But I discovered that my decision two years later to marry a former Jesuit would put an end to those hopes. On one level I could accept this as a consequence of my choices; I told myself I knew making that decision would mean the loss of many things I loved. But on another level, I experienced a deep anger at the church I had served for many years. Doors that had been wide open to me closed abruptly. Colleagues and friends apologized as they gave me news of job refusals and canceled talks. I found myself working in a bank to pay the rent, much to the chagrin of friends who had some realistic sense of my abilities. I embarrassed myself by bursting into tears when people asked me what I was doing with my life.

One day I realized that my anger was destroying me. I had to find creative ways to use it. I stopped focusing on what I was barred from doing, and asked myself what else there was that I loved and valued. What did I want to do that I had power to bring about? I began to write my first book. Each time I felt the bitterness and despair rise in me, I refocused on what I could do that would not be blocked and rejected. I returned to graduate school to pursue a social work degree, while doing substitute teaching. I broadened my concept of teaching to include new forms of ministry. I let myself grieve the world of university teaching as I had known it. This did not happen overnight; in fact, it took a number of years. But my anger began to subside as I clarified what I wanted and found ways to create it.

Bearing Witness through Works of the Imagination

Women, especially those whose lives are most marginalized, have had to fight continually for recognition. This has absorbed energy that might have been used for positive contributions to the world. But they have nonetheless continued to move forward. One way to subvert repression is by bearing witness through works of the imagination. This can begin with small steps. A principle of chaos theory discovered by meteorological scientist Edward Lorenz is that small events can have enormous consequences. Chaos science studies randomness, from that of the flow of weather and traffic to the unexpected movements in the solar system and galaxies. As a meteorologist, Lorenz had long suspected that very small causes have far-reaching results. This discovery is sometimes called "the butterfly effect." The movement of a butterfly wing in Asia affects the weather in New York a few days or weeks later.

Rather than bury their anger, some women transform it into literature or other forms of art. Women are exchanging their stories, writing newsletters, painting, staging plays, and producing other works of art. One example of such literature is the collaborative account Sandra Butler and Barbara Rosenblum write of their life together from the moment of the diagnosis of Barbara's breast cancer to her untimely death. The resulting book, *Cancer in Two Voices,* tells how her tumor was misdiagnosed time after time until it was too late for the medical profession to do anything but amputate her breast, bombard her with toxic chemicals, and use radiation to prolong her life for just three torturous years.[7] Such transforming of silence into language and action is not only a way of dealing with pain and rage. It is a gift to other women as well.

Such witness occurs in the face of even larger terrors. We now possess a body of imaginative literature that struggles to comprehend and describe the unparalleled evil of events such as the Holocaust. In *Writing As Resistance: Four Women Confronting the Holocaust*, Rachel Brenner examines the legacy of Edith Stein, Simone Weil, Anne Frank, and Etty Hillesum.[8] "We left the camp singing," wrote Etty Hillesum on a card thrown out of the train from Westerbork to Auschwitz on September 7, 1943. The Nazi scheme to annihilate European Jewry elicited responses, Brenner believes, that compel us to reconsider the meaning of resistance.

The four women who are the subjects of Brenner's study opposed Hitlerian tyranny through the act of writing. It is especially their autobiographical works that point to self-introspection as a mode of resistance. These texts were published long after their authors had died: Stein's autobiographical *Life in a Jewish Family* in 1965, Weil's "Spiritual Autobiography" and letters in the 1950s, Anne Frank's *Diary* in 1953, and Etty Hillesum's *Diary and Letters from Westerbork* in the 1980s. Their life narratives affirm solidarity with self, God, and others under the rule of terror that sought to dehumanize them.

Through a close examination of their writings, Brenner shows that the intellectual creativity of these four women presents a complex case of resistance. The reality of the Nazi anti-Jewish terror signified for them not only the horror of physical persecution, degradation, and annihilation; it was also a profound spiritual predicament. Their works reaffirm the ideal of human fellowship in the midst of global war and mass murder. "As paradoxical as it may seem, the autobiographical writings of these Jewish women doomed to death reflect a staunch yet not blindly naive belief in the humanistic creed as a guideline to the moral redemption of the world."[9] They are intensely preoccupied with the contemporary and future moral situation of humanity; this is the core of their defiance of terror. It stands in complete opposition to the Nazi design to deprive them of their humanity before extermination.

To preserve their courage the women need to reaffirm God, even if God has disappeared from the horizon. Each seeks communion with the Divine by a different path: Edith Stein desired to take up the cross for her people; Simone Weil sought to reach God through "decreation"; Anne Frank searched for a comforting God to be found in nature; and Etty Hillesum spoke of a weak and suffering God in need of our help. Yet each woman hopes that, in spite of the apparent disappearance of the Divine from the historical moment in which they are living, God will reappear in the future. Their legacy of creative resistance, the witness of their writings, is ultimately an affirmation of our humanity as a spark of the Divine.

21. The God Who Is in Fire: A Meditation on the Book of Ruth

> I, the fiery power, lie hidden in these things
> and they blaze from me.
>
> — Hildegaard of Bingen[1]

The opening sentences of the Book of Ruth draw us at once into a story of tragedy.[2] Famine stalks the land of Judah. It forces Naomi, her husband Elimelech, and their two sons, Mahlon and Chilion, to leave Bethlehem and migrate to Moab. But their fortunes worsen in this alien land. Naomi's husband dies. Her sons marry Moabite women, Orpah and Ruth. Then, ten years later, both sons perish as well. Now widowed and childless, Naomi gets word that there is once again food in Bethlehem. She decides it is time to return home.

Naomi sets out on her journey, accompanied by her two daughters-in-law. But she soon urges them to turn back and let her go on alone. Women can find security only in the house of a husband, and Naomi has no more sons to offer them. As she kisses Ruth and Orpah farewell, they begin to weep loudly. She blesses them:

> Go back each of you to your mother's house. May Yahweh be kind to you as you have been to those who have died and to me. (Ru 1:8)

In her blessing, Naomi invokes the loving-kindness of God, and her words carry echoes from the past: Yahweh hearing the cry of the Israelites in Egypt and being moved by their misery (Ex 3:7-8); God on the mountain with Moses, a God of mercy and steadfast love (Ex 34:6-7). But where has Naomi herself experienced this divine tenderness? Not near the sands of Egypt nor on any mountaintop. She has encountered the divine *chesed* hidden in family and friendship. It has come to her close at hand, in the faithful love of her daughters-in-law. She asks that God wrap these women in the same loving-kindness they have shown her.

Orpah eventually dries her tears and obeys Naomi. She returns to her people and her gods. But Ruth refuses; she will not be pushed away. She speaks with passionate and fierce loyalty.

> Do not press me to leave you and to turn back from your company, for wherever you go, I will go, wherever you live, I will live. Your people shall be my people, and your God, my God. (Ru 1:16)

Ruth embraces Naomi's God. And Ruth's very presence takes Naomi's dialogue with God to new levels. Ruth will lead Naomi out of darkness and show her the Divine as the true communion among persons. Together Ruth and Naomi are on a journey that neither could make alone. But it has a different meaning for each. For Naomi it is a return, through loss, grief, and anger, to a renewed hope. For Ruth, it is a venture into the unknown, to a people, a way of life, and a God different from all she has known.

Ruth clings to Naomi, the story tells us (Ru 1:14). Once again deeper levels of meaning resonate in these words. Naomi's ancestors were told repeatedly to cling to, hold fast to God (Dt 4:4; 11:22). God set before them life and death, blessing and curse. They are to choose life, loving and clinging to God, for that is where life and length of days are found (Dt 30:19–20). It is in the company of women that both Ruth and Naomi find this life. The love of friendship becomes a sacrament of the Divine.

> The two of them went on until they came to Bethlehem. Their arrival there set the whole town astir, and the women said, "Can this be Naomi?" (Ru 1:20)

When Naomi and Ruth arrive in Bethlehem, they produce a wave of excitement among the townswomen. Naomi's misfortunes have so altered her that her old friends and neighbors can hardly believe it is she. They gather round, and she somehow feels safe in their circle of interest and support. She pours her heart out to them, holding back nothing of the anger and despair she is feeling. As they hug her and welcome her back, they seem able to embrace a self she has come to despise.

How Naomi must have been flooded with memories on this return home: of herself as a contented wife and mother long ago; of Elimelech alive and strong; of Mahlon and Chilion young and healthy. Amid familiar landscapes, happier times course through her mind. But these are gone now. Her friends are right: She is not the same woman who left Judah a decade earlier. Life has seared and reduced her.

> But she said to them, "Do not call me Naomi, call me
> Mara, for Shaddai has marred me bitterly.
> Filled full I departed,
> Yahweh brings me back empty.
> Why call me Naomi, then,
> since Yahweh has given witness against me
> and Shaddai has afflicted me?" (Ru 1:20-22)

Naomi spits out her speech. She tells her old friends that the woman they knew no longer exists. Grief has killed her. True, the name *Naomi* means "pleasant or sweet one." But Naomi wants a new name, to match her inner reality, which is anything but pleasant. She is the bitter one, Mara, angry with the God who has stripped her of all that mattered. Her anger surges, powered by a sense of betrayal and the unfairness of her losses. The women are witnesses to her grievances against God.

Though Ruth is there with her, Naomi does not mention or introduce her, for she feels utterly alone with her sorrows. Ruth, who has risked everything to be faithful to her, is ignored. She seems able to handle this without letting it destroy their love. Ruth recognizes that Naomi's anger is not against her, but against an apparently arbitrary God. She understands that God can be the target of one's complaints and still be the source of one's redemption.

Who is this God who is the object of Naomi's anger, the God she blames for causing famine, dislocation, and death? El Shaddai is God almighty, God of the mountain, God the destroyer. But El Shaddai is also the one who told her ancestors to "be fruitful and multiply" (Gn 1:28), promising numerous descendants (Gn 17:1-2, 35:11). Naomi has known God both as the source of fertility and as its destroyer.

Naomi's story is set "in the days when the judges ruled" (Ru 1:1). It was a violent time. In the Book of Judges we read of a fiercely punishing God whose vengeance plays into power struggles between contending tribes and protects existing leaders from their enemies. This is God as Lord of warring hosts. Naomi learned to see both conquering enemies and devastating droughts as divine judgment on human sin, to find God in both blessing and curse.

Her anger is directed at this God who pronounces harsh judgments. Her suffering is like that of Job. But, unlike Job, she does not try to make sense of it through a direct dialogue with God. Nor is she reminded, as was Job, of human arrogance before the majesty of creation. Rather, as her sorrow and bitterness are received and held in a community of women, she somehow begins to heal. We are not told how she became whole and active again, but we see it happening in the story. Naomi's grief is the first step in her recovery; her anger gradually turns to wit and planning.

Naomi arrives in her homeland empty and bitter, but already there is a hint of hope: "And they came to Bethlehem at the beginning of the barley harvest" (Ru 1:22). The women welcome her and Ruth, their arms laden with sheaves of grain. Although this seasonal abundance now stands in stark contrast to the emptiness of Naomi's existence, it is an image of promise. The journey will yield distinctive harvests for both women as they mobilize their resources.

> Then Naomi, her mother-in-law, said to her, "My daughter, is it not my duty to see you happily settled?" (Ru 3:1)

We are hearing a woman's story set within a man's world. Ruth and Naomi must struggle for survival in a patriarchal environment. How will they provide for themselves? Neither is married, so neither has a husband to protect and feed her, to provide her with social status. But they are unconventional women; they carve a path between tradition and innovation. They do not succumb to the dangers and insecurities of their situation. Ruth refuses to give up and perish. Naomi does not stay stuck in bitterness; she will not let Ruth become prey to degradation and hunger. They make brave choices, using the power they possess.

Ruth and Naomi get active. Naomi devises a plan whereby Ruth will become appealing to Boaz, a wealthy farmer who is Naomi's kinsman. Ruth succeeds in pleasing Boaz, and he takes her for his wife. She bears a son who becomes the joy of Naomi's old age: "Then Naomi took the child and laid him in her bosom, and became his nurse" (Ru 4:16). No longer are they without family and shelter. God supports their efforts as they work out their salvation.

> "...for your daughter-in-law who loves you and is more to you than seven sons has given him birth...." And the women of the neighbourhood gave him a name. "A son has been born for Naomi," they said; and they named him Obed. This was the father of David's father, Jesse. (Ru 4:15–17)

The same chorus of voices that greets Naomi when she first returns in bitter emptiness now celebrates her with jubilation. The Book of Ruth begins and ends with a community of women embracing Ruth and Naomi in their bitterness and triumph, their emptiness and fullness. They lift up praise that is as superlative as it gets in a patriarchal culture, exclaiming to Naomi that Ruth is "more to you than seven sons" (Ru 4:15). Women and the outsider have moved from the periphery to the center. A poor, widowed foreigner becomes the great-grandmother of King David.

The brave and bold decisions of Naomi and Ruth both embody and bring about God's blessings. The Spirit of God that moved over the waters of creation is hidden but active in their lives. In a reversal of expectations, she who is from a despised people plays a privileged role in the story of salvation. Ruth and Naomi discover the power of connectedness, sustenance, healing, and creation. They stand as witnesses to a God of inclusiveness who wants all to flourish. They come to know Sophia, the God especially concerned with the poor, the suffering, and the outcast. Of them we might say: You are truly daughters of Wisdom, alive with the breath of God's power, acting with the strength She deploys from one end of the earth to the other (Wis 7:25; 8:34).

As we close the story of Ruth and Naomi, which reprises so many of the themes of this book, let us join with women everywhere, raising a chorus of blessing and hope:

> *Praise to you Spirit-Sophia, source of all transformation.*
> *Healing torn places, you give birth to change.*
> *In you, we create, find joy, make new beginnings.*
> *Hidden but moving, your signs are fire, wind, and water.*
> *Sister, mother, grandmother, lover, and friend,*
> *You keep us singing, hoping, believing, fiercely steadfast.*
> *Praise to you!*

NOTES

CHAPTER 1
CHOOSING TO FEEL

1. *At the Root of This Longing: Reconciling a Spiritual Hunger and a Feminist Thirst* (Harper San Francisco: 1998), 124.
2. *Meeting at the Crossroads: Women's Psychology and Girls' Development* (New York: Ballantine Books, 1992).
3. In *Making the Connections: Essays in Feminist Social Ethics*, ed. Carol S. Robb (Boston: Beacon Press, 1985), 3-21.
4. *Men, Women, and Aggression* (New York: HarperCollins, 1993), 1.
5. Ibid., 8.
6. (Freedom, Calif.: The Crossing Press, 1984), 129.

CHAPTER 2
DEEP NOTICING

1. *Ordinary Time: Cycles in Marriage, Faith, and Renewal* (Boston: Beacon Press, 1993), 11.
2. (New York: Harper & Row, 1985), 8.
3. Anne Klein discusses the importance of mindfulness for women in *Meeting the Great Bliss Queen: Buddhists, Feminists, and the Art of the Self* (Boston: Beacon Press, 1995), 61-88. See also her chapter entitled "Finding a Self: Buddhist and Feminist Perspectives," in *Shaping New Vision: Gender and Values in American Culture*, ed. Clarissa W. Atkinson, Constance H. Buchanan, and Margaret R. Miles (Ann Arbor, Mich.: UMI Research Press, 1987), 191-218.
4. (New York: HarperCollins, 1991), 94-107, 128-37, 168-82.
5. Translated in Nyanaponika Thera, *Heart of Buddhist Meditation* (London: Rider & Company, 1969), 114-15.
6. (San Diego: LuraMedia, 1989), 30.
7. See the discussion of Virginia Woolf in Jane Marcus, *Art and Anger: Reading Like a Woman* (Columbus: Ohio State University Press, 1988), 123-54.
8. Jean Baker Miller and Irene Pierce Stiver, *The Healing Connection:*

How Women Form Relationships in Therapy and in Life (Boston: Beacon Press, 1997), 134.

9. *Sands of the Well* (New York: New Directions, 1996), 107.

CHAPTER 3
EMOTIONAL INTERMISSIONS

1. *Otherwise: New and Selected Poems* (St. Paul, Minn.: Graywolf Press, 1996), 86.

2. (New York: Bell Tower, 1993), 146.

3. Thich Nhat Hanh, *Touching Peace: Practicing the Art of Mindful Living*, ed. Arnold Kotler (Berkeley, Calif.: Parallax Press, 1992), 16.

4. Mary Valentis and Anne Devane, *Female Rage: Unlocking Its Secrets, Claiming Its Power* (New York: Carol Southern Books, 1994), 207.

5. See Sandra Thomas and Cheryl Jefferson, *Use Your Anger: A Woman's Guide to Empowerment* (New York: Simon & Schuster, 1996), 26-27.

6. (New York: Random House, 1985), 203.

CHAPTER 4
BODY AND MIND

1. *Final Harvest: Emily Dickinson's Poems*, ed. Thomas H. Johnson (Boston: Little, Brown and Company, 1961), 278.

2. Mary Valentis and Anne Devane, *Female Rage: Unlocking Its Secrets, Claiming Its Power* (New York: Carol Southern Books, 1994), 207.

3. *Women's Bodies, Women's Wisdom: Creating Physical and Emotional Health and Healing* (New York: Bantam Books, 1994), 30.

4. *Female Rage*, 205.

5. *The Awful Rowing Toward God* (Boston: Houghton Mifflin, 1975), 26.

6. *Candles in Babylon* (New York: New Directions, 1982), 9.

7. *Our Cry for Life: Feminist Theology from Latin America* (Maryknoll, N.Y.: Orbis Books, 1993), 110-12.

8. See Eugene T. Gendlin, *Let Your Body Interpret Your Dreams* (Wilmette, Ill.: Chiron Publications, 1986), 67.

9. *Descartes' Error: Emotion, Reason, and the Human Brain* (New York: Avon Books, 1994), xvi.

10. *Otherwise: New and Selected Poems* (St. Paul, Minn.: Graywolf Press, 1996), 69.

11. On cognitive therapy, see Aaron T. Beck, *Love Is Never Enough: How Couples Can Overcome Misunderstandings, Resolve Conflicts, and Solve Relationship Problems through Cognitive Therapy* (New York: Harper & Row, 1988); and David Burns, *Feeling Good: The New Mood Therapy* (New York: Signet Books, 1980).

CHAPTER 5
MIXED EMOTIONS

1. *An Interrupted Life: The Diaries of Etty Hillesum 1941-43* (New York: Simon & Schuster, 1985), 159.

2. (New York: Penguin Books, 1994), 30.

3. See *Of Woman Born: Motherhood as Experience and Institution* (New York: W. W. Norton & Company, 1986), 21-23; and *The Fact of a Doorframe: Poems Selected and New 1950-1984* (New York: W. W. Norton & Company, 1981), 4.

4. *The Message of the Psalms: A Theological Commentary* (Minneapolis: Augsburg Publishing House, 1984), 19. Kathleen Norris has an insightful chapter on praying the psalms in *The Cloister Walk* (New York: Riverhead Books, 1996), 90-107. For a fine treatment of passion in God, including the interplay of divine anger and tenderness, see James D. and Evelyn Eaton Whitehead, *Shadows of the Heart: A Spirituality of the Negative Emotions* (New York: Crossroad, 1994).

5. See Kathleen A. Farmer, "Psalms," in *The Women's Bible Commentary*, ed. Carol A. Newsom and Sharon H. Ringe (Louisville, Ky.: Westminster John Knox Press, 1992), 137-44.

CHAPTER 6
THE HISTORY OF OUR FEELINGS

1. *Journeys by Heart: A Christology of Erotic Power* (New York: Crossroad, 1988), 22.

2. (Freedom, Calif.: The Crossing Press, 1984), 75-76.

3. A fine treatment of emotional memories can be found in Donna M. Orange, *Emotional Understanding: Studies in Psychoanalytic Epistemology* (New York: Guilford Press, 1995), 105-24.

4. (Boston: Beacon Press, 1997), 39-41, 74-79, 150.

5. New York: Penguin Books, 1987), 42.

6. *Trauma and Recovery: The Aftermath of Violence—From Domestic Abuse to Political Terror* (New York: Basic Books, 1992), 34.

7. See Katy Butler, "The Biology of Fear," *The Family Therapy Networker* (July/August 1996): 38-45.

8. Susan J. Brison, "Outliving Oneself: Trauma, Memory, and Personal Identity," in *Feminists Rethink the Self*, ed. Diana Tietjens Meyers (New York: HarperCollins, 1997), 32.

9. This description is from rabbinic literature as cited by Dale Moody, in "Shekinah," *The Interpreter's Dictionary of the Bible*, ed. G. A. Buttrick (Nashville: Abingdon Press, 1962), 4:318. See also Elizabeth A. Johnson, *She Who Is: The Mystery of God in Feminist Theological Discourse* (New York: Crossroad, 1992), 85-86.

CHAPTER 7
HOSTILITY AND COMMUNITY

1. *The Body of God: An Ecological Theology* (Minneapolis: Fortress Press, 1993), 62.

2. Frank Parchman, "Driven to Destruction," *Seattle Weekly*, December 31, 1997, 13-15.

3. For a summary of this research, see "Stress, Illness, and Your Heart—Myths of Suppressed Anger," in Carol Tavris, *Anger: The Misunderstood Emotion*, rev. ed. (New York: Simon & Schuster, 1989), 101-27.

4. See Anne Campbell, *Men, Women, and Aggression* (New York: HarperCollins, 1993), 41.

5. Linda Hogan, *Dwellings: A Spiritual History of the Living World* (New York: Simon & Schuster, 1996), 157.

6. (New York: Harcourt Brace & Company, 1995), 186.

CHAPTER 8
ANGER AND SELF-ESTEEM

1. Quoted by Maria Jose F. Rosado Nunes, "Women's Voices in Latin American Theology," in *The Power of Naming: A Concilium Reader in Feminist Liberation Theology*, ed. Elisabeth Schüssler Fiorenza (Maryknoll, N.Y.: Orbis Books, 1996), 14.

2. See *Focus On Women*, vol. 15: *Women and Anger*, ed. Sandra P. Thomas (New York: Springer, 1993), 101-4.

3. *Final Harvest: Emily Dickinson's Poems*, ed. Thomas H. Johnson (Boston: Little, Brown and Company, 1961), 135.

4. "No Defect Here: A Black Roman Catholic Womanist Reflection on a Spirituality of Survival," in *Defecting in Place: Women Claiming*

Responsibility for Their Own Spiritual Lives, ed. Miriam Therese Winter, Adair Lummis, and Allison Stokes (New York: Crossroad, 1995), 217-20.

5. In *Women in Praise of the Sacred: 43 Centuries of Spiritual Poetry by Women*, ed. Jane Hirshfield (New York: HarperCollins, 1994), 87. For more on Mechtild of Magdeburg, see *Beguine Spirituality: Mystical Writings of Mechtild of Magdeburg, Beatrice of Nazareth, and Hadewijch of Brabant*, ed. Fiona Bowie (New York: Crossroad, 1989); and Caroline Walker Bynum, *Jesus as Mother: Studies in the Spirituality of the High Middle Ages* (Berkeley: University of California Press, 1982).

6. On the use of the imagination in prayer, see Wilkie Au and Noreen Cannon, *Urgings of the Heart: A Spirituality of Integration* (Mahwah, N.J.: Paulist Press, 1995), 43-63; and Kathleen Fischer, *The Inner Rainbow: The Imagination in Christian Life* (Mahwah, N.J.: Paulist Press, 1983).

7. See Kathleen Norris's comments on Gregorian chant and plainsong in *The Cloister Walk* (New York: Riverhead Books, 1996), 329-31.

8. Paula Gunn Allen, *The Sacred Hoop: Recovering the Feminine in American Indian Traditions* (Boston: Beacon Press, 1986), 60-61.

9. Cited in Kat Duff, *The Alchemy of Illness* (New York: Bell Tower, 1993), 73.

10. (New York: Dell, 1983), 24.

11. Kathleen Fischer and Thomas Hart, *A Counselor's Prayer Book* (Mahwah, N.J.: Paulist Press, 1994), 90-91.

CHAPTER 9
GOOD GIRLS DON'T GET ANGRY

1. (London: Sheed & Ward, 1975), 118.

2. See Mary Collins, "Daughters of the Church: The Four Theresas," in *The Power of Naming: A Concilium Reader in Feminist Liberation Theology*, ed. Elisabeth Schüssler Fiorenza (Maryknoll, N.Y.: Orbis Books, 1996), 237. A fresh look at women saints can also be found in Elizabeth A. Johnson, *Friends of God and Prophets: A Feminist Theological Reading of the Communion of Saints* (New York: Continuum, 1998).

3. *Our Cry for Life: Feminist Theology from Latin America* (Maryknoll, N.Y.: Orbis Books, 1993), 172-77.

4. *Longing for Darkness: Tara and the Black Madonna* (New York: Viking Penguin, 1991), 15. See also China Galland, *The Bond Between Women: A Journey to Fierce Compassion* (New York: Penguin Putnam, 1998).

5. *Longing for Darkness*, 275.

6. *Our Lady of Guadalupe: Faith and Empowerment among Mexican-American Women* (Austin: University of Texas Press, 1994), 124, 129.

7. *The Collected Works of St. Teresa of Avila*, trans. Kieran Kavanaugh and Otilio Rodriguez, vol. 2: *The Way of Perfection, Meditations on the Song of Songs, The Interior Castle* (Washington, D.C.: Institute of Carmelite Studies, 1980), 283.

8. See *The Collected Works*, vol. 1: *The Book of Her Life, Spiritual Testimonies, Soliloquies* (Washington, D.C.: Institute of Carmelite Studies, 1976).

9. A helpful treatment of Teresa's life can be found in Victoria Lincoln, *Teresa: A Woman. A Biography of Teresa of Avila*, ed. Elias Rivers and Antonio T. de Nicolas (Albany: State University of New York Press, 1984).

10. (Princeton, N.J.: Princeton University Press, 1990).

11. *The Collected Works*, vol. 1, 84.

12. (New York: HarperCollins, 1991).

13. *Bird by Bird: Some Instructions on Writing and Life* (New York: Doubleday Dell, 1994), 28.

14. Translation of this passage is from Rosemary Radford Ruether, A Wise Woman: A Spiritual Mentor," *The Christian Century* 110 (February 17, 1993): 165.

CHAPTER 10

LEARNING HOW TO CREATE BOUNDARIES

1. *Unopened Letters* (New York: Sheep Meadow Press, 1996), 15.

2. Quoted in Anne Campbell, *Men, Women, and Aggression* (New York: HarperCollins, 1993), 3.

3. "The Human Situation: A Feminine View," in *Womanspirit Rising: A Feminist Reader in Religion*, ed. Carol P. Christ and Judith Plaskow (New York: Harper & Row, 1979), 37.

4. Helpful discussions of empathy can be found in Judith V. Jordan, Janet L. Surrey, and Alexandra G. Kaplan, "Women and Empathy: Implications for Psychological Development and Psychotherapy"; and Judith V. Jordan, "Empathy and Self Boundaries," in *Women's Growth in Connection: Writings from the Stone Center*, ed. Judith V. Jordan, Alexandra G. Kaplan, Jean Baker Miller, Irene P. Stiver, and Janet L. Surrey (New York: Guilford Press, 1991), 27-50 and 67-80.

5. Quoted in Judith V. Jordan, "Empathy and Self Boundaries," 78.

6. Judith V. Jordan, et al., "Women and Empathy," 30.

7. (New York: Harper & Row, 1985), 138.

CHAPTER 11
LOVE AND ANGER IN INTIMATE RELATIONSHIPS

1. In *Making the Connections: Essays in Feminist Social Ethics*, ed. Carol S. Robb (Boston: Beacon Press, 1985), 15.

2. See *Focus On Women*, vol. 15: *Women and Anger*, ed. Sandra P. Thomas (New York: Springer, 1993), 68-90.

3. On the importance of anger to relationships, see Jean Baker Miller and Janet Surrey, "Revisioning Women's Anger: The Personal and the Global," Work in Progress, no. 43 (Wellesley, Mass.: The Stone Center, 1990).

4. James R. Averill, "Studies on Anger and Aggression: Implications for Theories of Emotion," *American Psychologist* 38: 1145-60. For a summary of other research on the positive functions of anger, see Sandra P. Thomas, ed. *Women and Anger*, 10-11.

5. "The Power of Anger in the Work of Love," in *Making the Connections*, 14.

6. An excellent discussion of these issues can be found in Teresa Bernardez, "Women and Anger—Cultural Prohibitions and the Feminine Ideal," Work in Progress, no. 31 (Wellesley, Mass.: The Stone Center, 1988).

7. (New York: Simon & Schuster, 1993), 315.

8. *Why Marriages Succeed or Fail...and How You Can Make Yours Last* (New York: Simon & Schuster, 1994), 29.

9. Ibid., 59-61.

10. *Sands of the Well* (New York: New Directions, 1996), 78.

11. *Why Marriages Succeed or Fail*, 139.

12. Jean Baker Miller and Irene Pierce Stiver, *The Healing Connection: How Women Form Relationships in Therapy and in Life* (Boston: Beacon Press, 1997), 29.

CHAPTER 12
RECEIVING ANGER

1. *The Gift of Anger: A Call to Faithful Action* (Louisville, Ky.: Westminster John Knox Press, 1995), 1.

2. *Final Gifts: Understanding the Special Awareness, Needs, and Communications of the Dying* (New York: Bantam Books, 1997), 42-48.

CHAPTER 13
RESOLVING CONFLICTS

1. In *Celebrating Women: The New Edition*, ed. Hannah Ward, Jennifer Wild, and Janet Morley (Harrisburg, Pa.: Morehouse, 1995), 92.

2. For further discussion of these dimensions of conflict, see Jean Marie Hiesberger and William N. Hendricks, *Dealing with Conflict and Anger* (Shawnee Mission, Kans.: National Press Publications, 1996); Matthew McKay, Peter D. Rogers, and Judith McKay, *When Anger Hurts: Quieting the Storm Within* (Oakland, Calif.: New Harbinger Publications, 1989); and Sandra Thomas and Cheryl Jefferson, *Use Your Anger: A Woman's Guide to Empowerment* (New York: Simon & Schuster, 1996).

3. This approach is recommended by Hiesberger and Hendricks, *Dealing with Conflict and Anger*, 160.

4. *Touching Peace: Practicing the Art of Mindful Living*, ed. Arnold Kotler (Berkeley, Calif.: Parallax Press, 1992), 61–78.

CHAPTER 14
LOSS, ILLNESS, AND ANGER

1. *Spells for a Clear Vision* (London, Ontario, Canada: Brick Books, 1994), 35.

2. Sandy Shore, "Mother's Rage Brings Warning to Nichols Jury," *Seattle Times*, January 1, 1998, A4.

3. A very fine discussion of all aspects of grief can be found in Therese A. Rando, *How to Go On Living When Someone You Love Dies* (New York: Bantam Books, 1991).

4. *Otherwise: New and Selected Poems* (St. Paul, Minn.: Graywolf Press, 1996), 10.

5. Her research is reported in Judith S. Wallerstein and Sandra Blakeslee, *Second Chances: Men, Women, and Children a Decade After Divorce* (New York: Ticknor & Fields, 1989).

6. Rev. ed. (New York: Simon & Schuster, 1989), 304–5.

7. (New York: Bell Tower, 1993), 139.

8. *Kitchen Table Wisdom: Stories That Heal* (New York: Riverhead Books, 1996), 29–31.

1. "Editor's Note," in Brian Lanker, *I Dream a World: Portraits of Black Women Who Changed America*, ed. Barbara Summers (New York: Stewart, Tabori & Chang, 1989), 6.

2. (New York: Random House, 1991), 10-12.

3. *Emotion and Gender: Constructing Meaning from Memory*, ed. June Crawford, Susan Kippax, Jenny Onyx, Una Gault, and Pam Benton (Newbury Park, Calif.: SAGE Publications, 1992), 183.

4. See *Focus on Women*, vol. 15: *Women and Anger*, ed. Sandra P. Thomas (New York: Springer, 1993).

5. Jean Baker Miller, "Women and Power," in *Women's Growth in Connection: Writings from the Stone Center*, ed. Judith V. Jordan, Alexandra G. Kaplan, Jean Baker Miller, Irene P. Stiver, and Janet L. Surrey (New York: Guilford Press, 1991), 182-83. See also Bernard Loomer, "Two Conceptions of Power," *Process Studies* 6 (Spring 1976): 5-32.

6. "Lint on the Fringe of the Garment: Feminist Women's Survival in the Institutional Church," *Grail: An Ecumenical Journal* 13/2 (June 1997): 13. See also Pamela W. Darling, *New Wine: The Story of Women Transforming Leadership and Power in the Episcopal Church* (Boston: Cowley Publications, 1994).

7. Jean Baker Miller, "Women and Power," 184.

8. *Memories of God: Theological Reflections on a Life* (Nashville: Abingdon Press, 1995), 102-3.

9. *Defecting in Place: Women Claiming Responsibility for Their Own Spiritual Lives*, ed. Miriam Therese Winter, Adair Lummis, and Allison Stokes (New York: Crossroad, 1995), 103. In *Powers of the Weak* (New York: Alfred A. Knopf, 1980), Elizabeth Janeway analyzes the role those in subordinate positions, especially women, play in the reform of social power. She describes three powers of the weak: disbelief, coming together, and acting in pursuit of shared goals.

10. *Defecting in Place*, 108.

11. "Women's Difference and Equal Rights in the Church," in *The Power of Naming: A Concilium Reader in Feminist Liberation Theology* (Maryknoll, N.Y.: Orbis Books, 1996), 213-14.

12. For efforts to describe this kind of power, see Rita Brock, *Journeys by Heart: A Christology of Erotic Power* (New York: Crossroad, 1988); Anne Carr, *Transforming Grace: Christian Tradition and Women's Experience* (San Francisco: Harper & Row, 1988), 151-52; and Joan

Chittister, *Job's Daughters: Women and Power* (Mahwah, N.J.: Paulist Press, 1990).

13. Janet Walton, "Ecclesiastical and Feminist Blessing," in *The Power of Naming*, 290.

14. Hallie Iglehart, *Womanspirit: A Guide to Women's Wisdom* (San Francisco: Harper & Row, 1983), 146.

15. "Women and Anger—Cultural Prohibitions and the Feminine Ideal," Work in Progress, no. 31 (Wellesley, Mass.: The Stone Center, 1988), 5.

16. (New York: Harper & Row, 1985).

17. (New York: Simon & Schuster, 1995).

18. The Global Fund for Women, with offices in Palo Alto, California, is a global network of women and men committed to a world of equality and social justice. It works with women and provides them with the financial means to attain this vision.

CHAPTER 16
ENDING VIOLENCE AGAINST WOMEN

1. *She Who Is: The Mystery of God in Feminist Theological Discourse* (New York: Crossroad, 1992), 258.

2. Jaya Menon, "Pray for Assailant of Karate Nuns," *Seattle Times*, May 14, 1996, A3.

3. For an analysis of the problem, see *Violence and the Family: Report of the American Psychological Association Presidential Task Force on Violence and the Family* (Washington, D.C.: The American Psychological Association, 1996).

4. *Violence and the Family*, 112.

5. Neil Jacobson and John Gottman, *When Men Batter Women: New Insights into Ending Abusive Relationships* (New York: Simon & Schuster, 1998), 55–56, 268–69, 285–86. The comment by Jacobson is from Lauri Lowen, "Book by UW Psychologists Turns Spotlight on Domestic Abuse," *Jewish Transcript*, 74/13 (July 3, 1998): 11. See also Carol J. Adams, *Woman-Battering* (Minneapolis: Fortress Press, 1994); and Ann Jones and Susan Schechter, *When Love Goes Wrong: What to Do When You Can't Do Anything Right. Strategies for Women with Controlling Partners* (New York: HarperCollins, 1993).

6. See Susan Brooks Thistlethwaite, "Every Two Minutes: Battered Women and Feminist Interpretation," in *Feminist Interpretation of the Bible*, ed. Letty M. Russell (Philadelphia: Westminster Press, 1985),

96-110; and *Women Resisting Violence: Spirituality for Life,* ed. Mary John Mananzan, Mercy Amba Oduyoye, Elsa Tamez, J. Shannon Clarkson, Mary C. Grey, and Letty M. Russell (Maryknoll, N.Y.: Orbis Books, 1996).

7. See Phyllis Trible, *God and the Rhetoric of Sexuality* (Philadelphia: Fortress Press, 1978), 72-143.

8. Trans. Pritish Nandy, in *Wise Women: Over 2000 Years of Spiritual Writing by Women,* ed. Susan Cahill (New York: W. W. Norton & Company, 1996), 238.

9. For more on the household codes, see Elisabeth Schüssler Fiorenza, *In Memory of Her: A Feminist Theological Reconstruction of Christian Origins* (New York: Crossroad, 1983), 251-84; E. Elizabeth Johnson, "Ephesians," in *The Women's Bible Commentary,* ed. Carol A. Newsom and Sharon H. Ringe (Louisville, Ky.: Westminster John Knox Press), 338-42; and Sarah J. Tanzer, "Ephesians," in *Searching the Scriptures,* vol. 2: *A Feminist Commentary,* ed. Elisabeth Schüssler Fiorenza (New York: Crossroad, 1994), 325-48.

10. See Mary Rose D'Angelo, "Colossians," in *Searching the Scriptures,* 313-24.

11. Dorothee Sölle, *Creative Disobedience* (Cleveland: Pilgrim Press, 1995), 57.

12. *The Cry of Tamar: Violence Against Women and the Church's Response* (Minneapolis: Fortress Press, 1995), 248.

13. (New York: Harcourt Brace Jovanovich, 1992), 273-74.

14. "The Transformation of Suffering: A Biblical and Theological Perspective," in *Violence Against Women and Children: A Christian Theological Sourcebook,* ed. Carol J. Adams and Marie M. Fortune (New York: Continuum, 1995), 91.

15. See Marie M. Fortune, "Forgiveness: The Last Step," in *Violence Against Women and Children,* 201-6.

16. See Frederick W. Keene, "Structures of Forgiveness in the New Testament," in *Violence Against Women and Children,* 121-34.

17. *Texts of Terror: Literary-Feminist Readings of Biblical Narratives* (Philadelphia: Fortress Press, 1984), 108-9.

18. (San Francisco: Harper & Row, 1985), 158-59.

CHAPTER 17
FORGIVENESS

1. *My First White Friend: Confessions on Race, Love, and Forgiveness* (New York: Viking Penguin, 1996), 117.

2. (New York: Dell, 1961), 63.

3. *Ordinary Time: Cycles in Marriage, Faith, and Renewal* (Boston: Beacon Press, 1993), 29. Other helpful treatments of forgiveness can be found in Martha Alken, *The Healing Power of Forgiving* (New York: Crossroad, 1997); Doris Donnelly, *Learning to Forgive* (Nashville: Abingdon Press, 1979); Terry D. Hargrave, *Families and Forgiveness: Healing Wounds in the Intergenerational Family* (New York: Brunner/Mazel Publishers, 1994); Gregory L. Jones, *Embodying Forgiveness: A Theological Analysis* (Grand Rapids, Mich.: Eerdmans, 1995); and Jeffrie G. Murphy and Jean Hampton, *Forgiveness and Mercy* (Cambridge: Cambridge University Press, 1988).

4. Aruna Gnanadason, "Women and Spirituality in Asia," in *Feminist Theology from the Third World*, ed. Ursula King (Maryknoll, N.Y.: Orbis Books, 1994), 354–55.

5. Kirkridge is in Bangor, Pennsylvania. This excerpt is from *The Ridgeleaf* for May 1997.

6. *Woman, Earth and Spirit: The Feminine in Symbol and Myth* (New York: Crossroad, 1984), 99.

7. (Chicago: University of Chicago Press, 1958), 236–42.

8. *My First White Friend*, 2.

9. Ibid., 67.

10. The importance of this aspect of forgiveness is supported by the research of Steen Halling, Jan Rowe, and their colleagues in the Seattle University Department of Psychology. See Lin Bauer, et al., "Exploring Self-Forgiveness," *Journal of Religion and Health* 31 (1992): 149–60; and Jan O. Rowe, et al., "The Psychology of Forgiving Another: A Dialogal Research Approach," in *Existential-Phenomenological Perspectives in Psychology: Exploring the Breadth of Human Experience*, ed. R. S. Valle and S. Halling (New York: Plenum Publishing Corporation, 1989), 233–44.

11. See Matthew McKay, Peter D. Rogers, and Judith McKay, *When Anger Hurts: Quieting the Storm Within*, ed. Kirk Johnson (Oakland, Calif.: New Harbinger Publications, 1989), 84.

12. See Jean Marie Hiesberger and Dr. William N. Hendricks, *Dealing with Conflict and Anger* (Shawnee Mission, Kans.: National Press Publications, 1996), 13–15.

13. Florangela Davila, "Offenders Face Victims in Mediation," *Seattle Times*, March 11, 1996, B1-2.

14. Garry Cooper and Laurie Kahn, "Truth and Reconciliation: Healing the Wounds of Apartheid," *The Family Therapy Networker* 21/3 (May/June 1997): 14.

15. Ibid., 14.

16. Chung Hyun Kyung, "Your Comfort vs. My Death," in *Women Resisting Violence: Spirituality for Life*, ed. Mary John Maranzan, Mercy Amba Oduyoye, Elsa Tamez, J. Shannon Clarkson, Mary C. Grey, and Letty M. Russell (Maryknoll, N.Y.: Orbis Books, 1996), 137.

CHAPTER 18
LOVING ENEMIES

1. "Love Your Enemy: Sex, Power, and Christian Ethics," in *Feminist Theological Ethics: A Reader*, ed. Lois K. Daly (Louisville, Ky.: Westminster John Knox Press, 1994), 256.

2. Walter Wink, "The Third Way: Reclaiming Jesus' Nonviolent Alternative," *Sojourners* (December 1986): 28. See also his trilogy, *Naming the Powers, Engaging the Powers*, and *Unmasking the Powers* (Philadelphia: Fortress Press, 1984, 1992, 1993).

3. See Wink, "The Third Way," 30-31.

4. Kristin Jackson, "Give and Taken," *Seattle Times*, December 21, 1997, K1-2.

5. *The Gift of Fear: Survival Signals That Protect Us from Violence* (Boston: Little, Brown and Company, 1997), 65.

6. Ibid., 57.

7. See Antonio R. Damasio, *Descartes' Error: Emotion, Reason, and the Human Brain* (New York: Avon Books, 1994). For a helpful summary of new discoveries regarding the interplay of brain structures and emotions, see Daniel Goleman, *Emotional Intelligence* (New York: Bantam Books, 1995), 3-29.

8. (New York: Simon & Schuster, 1995), 151.

9. See Jack Kornfield, *A Path with Heart: A Guide through the Perils and Promises of Spiritual Life* (New York: Bantam Books, 1993), 19-21; and Mary Jo Meadow, *Gentling the Heart: Buddhist Loving-Kindness Practice for Christians* (New York: Crossroad, 1994).

CHAPTER 19
WOMEN AND NONVIOLENT RESISTANCE

1. *You Can't Kill the Spirit* (Philadelphia: New Society Publishers, 1988), 7. See also *Reweaving the Web of Life: Feminism and Nonviolence*, ed. Pam McAllister (Philadelphia: New Society Publishers, 1982); and Cambridge Women's Peace Collective, *My Country Is the Whole World: An Anthology of Women's Work on Peace and War* (Boston: Pandora Press, 1984).

2. *You Can't Kill the Spirit*, 21. My description is based on McAllister's account on pp. 20-24, along with Jo Fisher, in *Mothers of the Disappeared* (Boston: South End Press, 1989); and Elizabeth Hanly, "A Seventh Year of Unknowing: The Witness of Argentina's Mothers of the Plaza de Mayo," *Sojourners* (April 1983): 21-25.

3. "A Seventh Year of Unknowing," 22.

4. Ibid., 23.

5. "Remembering Who We Are," in *We Are Part of One Another: A Barbara Deming Reader*, ed. Jane Meyerding (Philadelphia: New Society Publishers, 1984), 288-90; and *You Can't Kill the Spirit*, 6.

6. Mohandas K. Gandhi, *An Autobiography: The Story of My Experiments with Truth* (Boston: Beacon Press, 1957), 318-19, 350, 503-4.

7. *Gandhi on Non-Violence: Selections from the Writings of Mahatma Gandhi*, ed. Thomas Merton (New York: New Directions, 1965), 37.

8. *You Can't Kill the Spirit*, 4-5.

9. Gene Sharp, *The Politics of Nonviolent Action*, Part 2: "The Methods of Nonviolent Action" (Boston: Porter Sargent Publishers, 1973). Sharp lists nearly two hundred nonviolent tactics, but gives few examples of women's action.

10. "The Good Housekeeping Award: Women Heroes of Environmental Activism," *Sojourners* (July-August 1997): 26.

11. Katie Geneva Cannon, "Surviving the Blight," in *My Soul Is a Witness: African-American Women's Spirituality*, ed. Gloria Wade-Gayles (Boston: Beacon Press, 1995), 23.

12. Lisa Pertillar Brevard, "'Will the Circle Be Unbroken': African-American Women's Spirituality in Sacred Song Traditions," in *My Soul Is a Witness*, 40-41.

13. *Reading Ruth: Contemporary Women Reclaim a Sacred Story*, ed. Judith A. Kates and Gail Twersky Reimer (New York: Ballantine Books, 1994), xvii.

CHAPTER 20
ANGER AND CREATIVITY

1. In *Wise Women: Over Two Thousand Years of Spiritual Writings by Women,* ed. Susan Cahill (New York: W. W. Norton & Company, 1996), 222.

2. Cristina Igoa, "Immigrant Children: Art as a Second Language," in *Invisible Children in the Society and Its Schools,* ed. Sue Books (Mahwah, N.J.: Lawrence Erlbaum Associates, 1998), 67-88; and Cristina Igoa, *The Inner World of the Immigrant Child* (New York: St. Martin's Press, 1995).

3. For reflections on the new science, see Kitty Ferguson, *The Fire in the Equations: Science, Religion and the Search for God* (Grand Rapids, Mich.: Eerdmans, 1994); and Danah Zohar, *The Quantum Self: Human Nature and Consciousness Defined by the New Physics* (New York: William Morrow, 1990).

4. *Female Rage: Unlocking Its Secrets, Claiming Its Power* (New York: Carol Southern Books, 1994), 216.

5. *The Book of Blessings: New Jewish Prayers for Daily Life, the Sabbath, and the New Moon Festival* (Harper San Francisco, 1996), 174, 288, 166.

6. *Women's Bodies, Women's Wisdom: Creating Physical and Emotional Health and Healing* (New York: Bantam Books, 1994), 63ff.

7. (San Francisco: Spinsters Book Company, 1991).

8. *Writing As Resistance: Four Women Confronting the Holocaust* (University Park: The Pennsylvania State University Press, 1997).

9. Ibid., 9.

CHAPTER 21
THE GOD WHO IS IN FIRE:
A MEDITATION ON THE BOOK OF RUTH

1. In *Hildegaard of Bingen: Mystical Writings,* trans. Robert Carver, ed. Fiona Bowie and Oliver Davies (New York: Crossroad, 1990), 93.

2. My reading of the Book of Ruth has been shaped by the following sources: Katheryn Pfisterer Darr, *Far More Precious Than Jewels: Perspectives on Biblical Women* (Louisville, Ky.: Westminster John Knox Press, 1991), 55-84; June Jordan, "Ruth and Naomi, David and Jonathan: One Love," in *Wise Women: Over Two Thousand years of Spiritual Writings by Women,* ed. Susan Cahill (New York: W. W. Norton & Company, 1996), 247-51; Amy-Jill Levine, "Ruth," in *The Women's Bible*

200